I hate to complain, but ...

I hate to complain, but ...

A Collection of Humorous Something-or-others by

Jim Foster

THE DUNDURN GROUP
A HOUNSLOW BOOK
TORONTO · OXFORD

Publisher: Anthony Hawke
Editor: Barry Jowett
Design: Jennifer Scott
Cover illustration by Anthony Jenkins
Printer: Transcontinental Printing Inc.

Canadian Cataloguing in Publication Data
Foster, Jim (James E.)
I hate to complain, but —
ISBN 0-88882-214-6
1. Canadian wit and humor (English).* I. Title.
PS8561.O77427I32 1999   C818'.5402   C99-932277-X
PR9199.3.F5725I32 1999

1   2   3   4   5   03   02   01   00   99

THE CANADA COUNCIL | LE CONSEIL DES ARTS
FOR THE ARTS | DU CANADA
SINCE 1957 | DEPUIS 1957

We acknowledge the support of the **Canada Council for the Arts** for our publishing program. We also acknowledge the support of the **Ontario Arts Council**, and we acknowledge the financial support of the Government of Canada through the **Book Publishing Industry Development Program** (BPIDP) for our publishing activities.

Care has been taken to trace the ownership of copyright material used in this book. The author and the publisher welcome any information enabling them to rectify any references or credit in subsequent edidtions.

J.Kirk Howard, President

Printed and bound in Canada. Printed on recycled paper.

Dundurn Press
8 Market Street
Suite 200
Toronto, Ontario, Canada
M5E 1M6

Dundurn Press
73 Lime Walk
Headington, Oxford,
England
OX3 7AD

Dundurn Press
2250 Military Road
Tonawanda, New York
U.S.A. 14150

table of contents ...

introduction

I have no idea why I'm sitting here at 4:33 on a Saturday morning starting a book.

This won't be the great Canadian novel by the way. It's a collection of past columns (the ones I liked). This time they haven't been edited by the boys in the newsroom. I'm not complaining, they were kind most of the time and left my stuff alone. I think I'm a lot like the tribal idiot in a primitive culture. The rest of the group never quite knew what would happen if they crossed him. Once or twice, Jeff Day, the managing editor, slashed a few lines, but rarely, and if he did it was usually because I had committed some minor journalistic sin — like mentioning a rival paper. According to Jeff, competition is tough enough these days without giving the opposition free publicity. Actually there was more to his reasoning. There appears to be some sort of understanding among the local news gatherers up here in the backwoods not to go at each other. The whole thing could very well end up in a peeing contest between E-Z Rock, The New VR, the *Orillia Today*, and of course, the mighty *Packet*.

I have been absolutely amazed at how far these columns have travelled. Friends have mailed them all over the place. Sue and Bruce Waite sent them to the late Dr. Ralph Curry in Tennessee. Joan and Doc Wensley sent a few to Saudi Arabia. I got a letter from Vancouver once about something I wrote — fairly flattering, if I remember. (How it got to B.C. I have no idea. Perhaps someone used it to wrap a whitefish and dropped in a mailbox.) Cay MacDonald passes them on to her daughter-in-law, Linda Leatherdale, the business editor of the *Toronto Sun*.

I have no idea whether the Queen gets a copy dropped on her breakfast tray every Tuesday morning, or whether the poor dear has to wait until some local Royalist checks the *Packet* for anti-British sentiment before passing it along.

Actually that was a stupid statement. Of course the Queen gets her own copy. How else could Liz keep up with the goings on at the Orillia Council meetings? I'm sure that many a morning she's leaned over and whispered, "Phil, are you awake? You'll never guess what those bozos on Andrew Street did this time."

I am not a journalist, or a newspaper man. Years ago I worked at the flagship of Gordon E. Smith's publishing empire, the *Beaverton Express*, a weekly with a circulation that probably left the *New York Times* green with envy. I never wrote a word. Had I taken pen in hand and wrote a column back in the early Sixties, Gord would have gone to jail instead of Queen's Park.

It's fun hanging around the *Packet*, though. I sit way up by the publisher's office door. I used to think it was because Ken Koyama liked me handy in case he needed my insight into some of the more complex political problems of the day. Or he might need someone to decipher the ravings of my fellow scribes, Pete McGarvey, Kate Grigg, and Bill Keller. But alas, I soon realized that I'm there so he can keep an eye on me.

I miss Randy Richmond. Randy was the news editor when I started. He had the nerve to say what he thought about the local political disasters, although I'm sure that the *Packet*'s lawyers earned their retainer. I could never get up enough nerve to write what I really thought about the actions (or inaction) of folks I could very well drink beer with the next day. Randy did. Half the city wanted him knighted and the other half wanted him boiled in oil. But Randy moved on to the *London Free Press*. Jeff went to the *Hamilton Spectator*. John Remington Size caught a bus and now toils away for the *North Bay Nugget*. Tom Villemaire just disappeared one day. I was standing there talking to him and "poof" he was gone. Thirty seconds later he was the Managing Editor of the *Collingwood Enterprise-Bulletin*. Newspaper people never seem to stay in one place too long. I suspect that they are part gypsy. They seem to drift from paper to paper until eventually they end up in a stack of old newspapers in Conrad Black's basement.

One of the most memorable days of my life (although for some reason I can't remember any of it) was spent out at the Leacock Home with the gang from the *Packet* and a pack of reporters and columnists from the *Toronto Sun*. I sat in the Boathouse for a delightful few hours talking to Andy Donato — one of Canada's greatest political cartoonists — and Max Haines — the mystery writer. Linda Leatherdale was there. I thought she would want to pick my brains for some investment advice, but all I remember her saying to me was, "I hope you aren't driving home. By the way, how did you lose your shoes anyway?"

I'm rambling. If you are from Orillia, you might remember some of these columns. If not, you'll probably wonder what sort of weirdos live up here in the sleepy little town of Mariposa. The city is full of them. Leacock didn't write about Orillia because we were dull. He realized very quickly that there must be something strange leaking into the drinking water that causes what appear to be normal human beings to act like they are all goofed up on mind-altering drugs or magic mushrooms.

The *Packet* did their bit a few years ago to add to this insanity by running a column called the "Talk of the Town." It was a brilliant concept that allowed anyone with an axe to grind, or a half-baked idea to share, to phone a hotline number and the paper would print it — without the caller having to identify him or herself, or even show proof of mental competency. I believe the same thing was tried at the *Salem Bugle* during the Witch Trials with much the same result. It was a wonderful source of columns and I was all for it until a few misfits felt it necessary to criticize my own deathless prose. Except for a minor tic I've developed, and the inability to fall asleep without an armed guard by my bed, I have managed to survive their critiques.

Alas, "Talk of the Town" is gone. I never really knew why it disappeared — threats of fire-bombing perhaps. The more clever readers have gone back to writing letters to the editors. The others have invested in books of voodoo spells and wile away the hours poking pins in little rag dolls that look remarkable like Mark Bisset, the rest of the gang in the newsroom, and the prettier ones, like me.

I'm not going to thank a whole pile of people. There are too many. I have to mention Pete McGarvey of course, and Doug Sneyd who sends my stuff to *Playboy*. *Playboy* pays in American money. I can't forget Dave Broadfoot, who is convinced that I have a sense of humour, although somewhat half-baked. He has also suggested that I need a psychiatric assessment. And my family of course, who demand it.

But most of all, I'd better mention my long-suffering wife, Sharon, who unfortunately understands me. Which is why her divorce lawyer's number is programmed into our phone.

Enough ... join me in a Feast of Foster

I'd better start with "Welcome to our hospital, Mr. Premier." It won the Ontario CP and Western Ontario Newspaper Awards for humour for 1996. It doesn't take too many brains to figure out why I wrote this one.

Welcome to our hospital, Mr. Premier
September 24, 1996

- Good morning Mr. Premier.
    - Good morning Ernie. Wait a minute. Where am I?
    - You're at Soldiers' Memorial Hospital, Mike. You're a very sick boy.
    - Tell me about it, I feel awful. What am I doing in a hospital?
    - We had to take your appendix out.
    - You what? My appendix? I had it out when I was a kid. What did they take out?
    - I have no idea, but it was red. I know it wasn't your heart because you haven't got one. Ask Dave Johnson, he did the surgery. I was just the anaesthetist.
    - Johnson? He's not a doctor. He's a ... come to think of it I don't know what he is. Where are the doctors?
    - None of them will work on you, Mike. They think you're a jerk. They said to let Jim Wilson fix you. He's the Health Minister. Let him make the twenty bucks.
    - I'm the premier of Ontario. What do you mean they won't work on me? I want to see a doctor.
    - It's Sunday. There's only one guy on call and he's working on some old geezer who was poisoned. The poor old guy drank some coffee out of that machine in the Emergency ward.
    - We'll see about that. Who in hell is in charge around here?
    - Some guy by the name of Penwarden, but he can't help you. He's up on Soldiers Two, washing the floor. We cut him back pretty bad, Mike ... had to lay off half his people. He should be down in a while. He has to come this way anyway to change all the lightbulbs to twenty-five watt.
    - My stomach's sore. Where's Dave Johnson ?
    - He's up in Obstetrics delivering a baby. He'll be making his rounds later. By the way Mike, he doesn't have any malpractice insurance. If you have any problems, you'll have to try and collect through his CAA.
    - This is ridiculous. My stomach hurts ... and my head. Why does my head hurt?

- I don't know anything about anaesthetics, Mike. I had to put you out, so I hit you on the head with a rock. By the way, don't move around very much, we stitched you up with some binder twine from Big Al McLean's farm.

- This is insane. Get me a nurse.

- There aren't any. To save money, they've had to go to someone that's a little less qualified. Someone who can do the job but doesn't quite have the same degree of medical training.

- Like who?

- Well, the girl who worked with Dave up in O.R. is a toothpaste mechanic at Shopper's, but she watches old reruns of Ben Casey to keep up with the new techniques. There was a good one this week about leeches. Look, don't panic Mike, this may work out all right. Once this is all over, Dave and I have been offered a job at a big hospital in Tennessee. We'll need it. We sure as hell won't get elected again.

- Tennessee? Why don't you stay here?

- Are you nuts? We're not working for this kind of money. Look, roll over. I've got to take your temperature. This is going to hurt a bit. I can't find the keys to the medicine cabinet to get one of their thermometers, so I have to use this one I took off the wall outside. Once we get it in past the Coke bottle picture, it should be fairly easy.

- My arm's sore. Why is my arm sore?

- I had to take your blood pressure. I didn't know when to stop pumping that little rubber bulb, so I just pumped until your fingers swelled up.

- Ernie, is there any chance you are after my job?

- Of course not, Mike. Why would you think such a thing?

- Oh nothing ... get your foot off my oxygen hose. Look, help me up. I'm getting out of here.

- Here, put your arm around my shoulder and I'll ...

- Ouch ... I can't move. I'm stuck here.

- Just a sec ... look Mike. We may have a little problem here.

- What now?

- I think Dave may have gone in a little deep with the stitches. I think he's sewed you to the table.

- Well cut them and get me out of here.

- Sorry, I can't Mike.

- You can't? Why in hell not?

but...

     - I'm off duty. You'll have to wait until the night nurse comes in.

     - Who's the night nurse?

     - Lynn McLeod. By the way, I'd brace myself if I were you. She doesn't love you like we do.

I believe this was from Galoshes 1:14.

Behold The Harris and His Kingdom
December 10, 1996

And it came to pass in the Land of Ontario, that an edict went out to all the people, that every person in the land shouldst choose the wisest from amongst their peers to journey unto the Six-Cities, that they should ponder together in the Great Hall of the Rulers.

For it is written, that a Grinch shall come down from the Land of Eternal Snows and Blackflies and He shall be called The Harris, and shall sit upon the great throne of the people, and His word shall be The Law.

Yea did the Grinch assemble his henchpersons and looketh over the great list of lawyers and used car dealers, and from amongst them did He name a council of disciples to carry out His bidding and to rule wisely ... or rule, anyway.

And He did bestow upon them great wisdom, e'en though they had little to begin with, and He did grant them vast powers over all that had cast their ballots. And the People did shake their heads in wonderment at their own stupidity ... including me.

Verily, did they do as was His command, and like gangbusters they did slash vast quantities of gold from the social programs. They choppest the welfare and behold, four and twenty deadbeats were removed from the roles. And four and twenty thousand good folk also, but they were but peasants, and matter not until the time of the electing is nigh. Then shall The Harris find big bucks to appease them ... those who didn't starve to death.

He did appointeth a sage from Clan Snobelin, who had studied e'en up to the tenth grade, and charged that he should revamp the great school systems, which did scareth the poop out of the educators and anyone else with half a mind.

He did send a Johnson to lay waste the followers of OPSEU and they did fight a mighty battle in the Six-Cities, yea, e'en to the very steps of the buildings of the rulers. And Big Al did place the Hat of Three Corners upon his head and did send in the cavalry and the rebels did fall back and lick their wounds.

But the Leah, who ruleth the people of OPSEU, did conspire with her allies and verily did they shutteth down the great cities.

They laid seige the City, London, stronghold of the Western lands, and to the East, Peterborough, where the bars stay open till nine o'clock, and to the South, Hamilton, in the land of the Copps and eternal smoke.

Finally, they did set upon the great Six-Cities and they strucketh the subways, the buses, e'en unto the carriages of the sick and the lame. And the street vendors did cry out and the merchants and the money-changers did shake their fists at the sky.

But The Harris did stand His ground, neither did He flinch, but did crack wise to the scribes and mock the people of the unions.

And The Harris saw the pain in the eyes of his subjects and was well pleased.

And in a twinkling, the Prince of Darkness did come to Him on the back nine and sayeth,

"Ye shall gather thy flunkies and yet shall ye declare that the merchants shall open their shops upon the Day of the Boxing. And the fur-traders shall rejoice, since they will be wintering in the Islands and shall now rest soundly as their minions are slogging to the marketplace, nether cheeks in snow. So shall they assign the duties to permanent part-timers, that they shall be paid but minimum wage and neither shall they receivest of benefits, and the cash registers shall ring and the taxes shall be four-fold and the bankers shall rub their hands in greed and celebration."

And the Grinch didst appoint a Wilson to cleanest up the Health-Care System as to follow that of the mighty United States which worketh not at all. But the silly ass did layeth waste the whole damn thing until the healers all moved to Tennessee and heart attacks had to be scheduled through the Ministry.

He did sell out the nurses, and did leave the sick and infirm in the hands of faith healers and other wackos. The young mothers shall birth their children at home ... or in a manger as it was the day The Harris was born.

And The Harris did realize that He had gone too far, and tooketh a one stroke penalty, then set upon the Workers Compensation Board. He didst chop the benefits of the injured that they should limp back to work or starve.

And The Harris looked over His works and saw that they were good.

But in a deep sleep, as He did dream of dumping the LCBO and the mighty Hydro and of the firing of the highway inspectors, a vision came unto him and the Angel of the People appeared before

but...

him saying, "There shall soon be'eth a Day of Reckoning and the people shall rise up against thee, and send thee scurrying back to the Bay, wagging thy tail behind thee. Michael, thou art not God."

What's the sense of being a senator if you have to go to work every day?

Picking on senator going too far
February 24, 1998

I rarely get involved with politics. Oh I might say something spiteful about Mike Harris or one of his henchmen, but that's different. Somehow the provincial government went from an average bunch of bozos to the most amazing collection of financial geniuses in the free world merely by being elected. I find that fascinating. I don't have much to say about the Feds, probably because I figure they are stumbling along as best they can with their limited intelligence.

I don't say much about Bill Clinton either. For one thing, it's none of my business who he is fooling around with. If Hillary wants to break his neck, that's up to her, but I can live without hearing about it twenty-four hours a day.

But I'm afraid I have to take a moment and speak up in defence of poor Andrew Thompson. I can't believe that the Canadian senators would suspend one of their own just because he missed a few days at the old salt mine. Now I realize that he was supposed to drop by for a visit last week, but the man was ill. At least he called in. There's a lot of flu bugs floating around. I think it is commendable that he thought enough of his fellow senators to keep his diseases to himself. I don't know what he had, but I suspect it was Montezuma's Revenge. (Mexico is the only country in the world where the expression "Royal Flush" has nothing to do with playing cards.) But what if Andy had shown up and infected the whole Senate? Then they would be coughing, sneezing, or running to the john all day, instead of sleeping in their benches like they usually do. A fat lot of good they would do for the country if they didn't get a good day's sleep. There's nothing worse than a grumpy senator. Look what a mess Joe McCarthy made in the States, and he was healthy. Although I believe he suffered from irregularity.

Some folks have even been mean enough to suggest that Andy wasn't even sick. I think that can be cleared up by simply asking him to bring in one of those little doctor's slips that say,

"Mr./Mrs. (check one)_____ was in my office today. He/she says he/she has:
___ a cold, ___ influenza, ___ bubonic plague, ___ loose smut of

oats, ___ iron deficiency anemia, ___ dandruff. (check one)
Dr._____
That will be $15.00 please."

On the other hand he may not be sick at all. He may be too embarrassed to come in ... or lonely. After all, he isn't likely to know anybody. He hasn't been there often enough to remember all their names. Worse still, he may have forgotten how to get there. I've been to Ottawa lots of times and I get lost once I hit the city limits. After all, if you've only been to a place seven times in fourteen years, you can hardly be expected to remember how to get there. We go to Petrolia five or six times every year, and I still have to use a road map. Of course Petrolia isn't a place that you want to hurry back to. Petrolia only has three donut shops in the whole town. The average Orillian wouldn't last an hour in a primitive culture like that. There's an OPP detachment there. I have no idea what the cops do. They probably have a kettle and a jar of instant. A cop would rather be caught without his revolver than without a cup of coffee in his hand. When officers graduates from Police College they are given a gun, a badge, and a discount card from Timmy Hortons which entitles them to ten cents off on a coffee or a bag of day-old donuts.

I don't know how I got from the Canadian Senate to the policing problems of Petrolia.

I have never quite figured out just exactly what it is that a Canadian senator is supposed to do. But whatever it is I would like to do it. We make big bucks writing columns here at the *Packet*, which makes you wonder why on any given day you can see us sitting on the front steps selling pencils out of a tin cup, but we certainly don't make 75,000 smackers a year. For that kind of money I'd be willing to show up once or twice a week and even stay all day if they serve lunch.

The more I think about it, I'm going to speak to Paul Devillers, our M.P., about an appointment. He's got a lot of drag in Ottawa because he is bilingual. I'm not, but that doesn't matter. As a senator I can sleep just as well in English as some Quebecer can in French. Paul will be glad to recommend me because I'm the only person in the riding that pronounces his name right. Besides, if any political party owes me a favour, it's the Liberals. I told everybody I was a Conservative. If that didn't get them a pile of votes nothing did.

One more column on Clinton's problems.

Some things "just happen"
January 27, 1998

I have no idea whether Bill Clinton was, or is, paddling around in the steno pool. I think we can be reasonably sure, however, that we won't ever find him in a gay bar. Strangely enough, unlike everyone else in the world, I don't think it's any of my business. The only reason I bring the subject up is because of one of the key players, Linda Tripp. A correspondent from Washington said that when Miss Tripp worked in the White House, she "just happened" to see some girl named Kathleen Willys leave the Oval Office with her lipstick smeared. She also "just happened" to befriend Monica Lewinsky, the latest alleged object of Bill's affections, and "just happened" to tape record her phone conversations and "just happened" to give them to lawyer, Kenneth Starr — all in the interest of National Security, of course. How would you like to have a nosy little witch like that for a friend?

Now she works in the Publicity Department of the Pentagon. It doesn't take too many brains to see that somewhere down the road, she will "just happen" to see some girl coming out of a general's office with her blouse on backwards, or "just happen" to discover that some admiral had more than a rubber ducky with him in the bathtub. I can see what happened now:

- Good morning Miss Tripp.
- Good morning Mr. President.
- New dress?
- What do you mean by that Mr. President?
- Nothing, Miss Tripp. You go by here every day. I just never noticed you wearing that dress before.
- You make it a habit of staring at all the women who work here in the White House?
- Well no, Miss Tripp, I was just trying to make conversation.
- And why is that Mr. President? Are you chatting me up, trying to get me into the Oval Office so you can have your way with me?
- Way with you? Miss Tripp, all I said was "good morning."
- Do you expect me to believe that? I've seen the way you look at me. I've seen the lust in your eyes. You think because you are the

President of the United States, I'll just crumble at your feet. I know all about your kind. I know all about men, Mr. Clinton. When I was born, I saw the way the doctor looked at me. As soon as I was able to talk, I turned him in to the AMA. He's still in the slammer. Then I turned in my Grade 1 teacher, I could see what she was doing with that plasticine. I had her fired. And when I was a cheerleader, I knew what the football team was thinking; I turned them all in. You men are all alike. I can't help it if I'm beautiful. It's a curse Bill, a curse. I know you can't control yourself whenever I walk by. Some of us just have it. What is it, Bill, my body, my golden hair, my long shapely legs? Oh Bill, don't fight it. I'm all woman. Take me Bill, right here in the hall. Just wait until I loosen my hair and set up my camcorder ... Oh Bill, carry me off to your office, your bedroom, your broom closet. Don't be shy. We were made for each other. Every time I look at you I can hear music, Bill. "All of me, why not take all of me? Can't you see ..."

- Aah, Miss Tripp. Um ... would you like a glass of water? You look a little flushed.

- Oh Bill, my darling, of course I'm flushed. My heart is pounding, pounding. Together we will sail off into the sunset. Can't you hear the music darling? "Love is a many splendoured thing. In the morning mist, two lovers kissed and the earth "

- Now Miss Tripp, I'm sure that you are a very nice lady and if I was a single man, I would ask you to have a coffee or something, but right now, I'm married and Hillary would kill me. Please don't take your jacket off, Miss Tripp. Don't Linda.

- You called me Linda. Oh Bill, you do love me. Come on down to the War Room, my sweet and I'll show you what carpet bombing is all about.

- Miss Tripp, please. Now put your clothes back on. Yes that's a lovely tattoo and every time I see a rose, I'll certainly think of you. Just calm down. Now Linda, I'm just going to call security. No don't stand up in front of that window Miss Tripp, it faces out onto Pennsylvania Avenue. SECURITY! HELP! Now calm down Linda. Here, put my jacket around your shoulders. Please, Linda, stay away from me. Now stay calm here they come now.

- SECURITY! THANK GOD YOU'RE HERE. THE PRESIDENT ATTACKED ME.

Or something like that.

I wrote this after I had lunch at the Leacock Museum and Charlie Baillie of the TD was sitting there. If he had bought me a beer, I might have seen his side of the big bank merger.

Merger mania makes him nervous
April 21, 1998

Why am I not ecstatic because the T.D. and the C.I.B.C. banks have announced their engagement? For some reason it reminds me of Neville Chamberlain's "Peace in our time" speech. I listened to the two presidents, Al Flood and our own Charlie Baillie, explain what a glorious thing it will be for the consumer. But somehow I got the same feeling I got when Doc McAlister said, "While your curled up there Jimbo, we might as well check the old prostate."

I can imagine old Stevie Leacock walking into the T.D.C.I.B.C. today and trying to open an account with his fifty-six bucks. By the time he got out the door, he would be penniless and the bank would own his house, his rowboat and have first dibs on Stevie Jr.

With apologies to Stephen:

When I go into a bank, I get rattled. For one thing I usually go in on Friday. Friday at the bank is a freak show ... dress-down day. The staff wear anything from Parisian designer leisure suits, to pink track pants that normal people wouldn't use for paint rags.

My salary at the *Packet* had been raised to a hefty fifty dollars a month for writing a weekly column, doing the *Seniors Magazine*, emptying the garbage, and certain technical duties which involve a pail of water, a sponge, and Ken Koyama's car, and I felt that the bank was the only place for it.

For some reason, I had an idea that a person about to open an account needs consult the manager.

I went up to a counter marked "Reception" and asked to speak to the manager.

The lady behind the desk said, "We don't have a manager. We have Customer Service Officers, Financial Analysts, Investment Counsellors, Tax Advisors, Personal Bankers, Small Business Consultants, Lending Officers, Mortgage Specialists, Chartered Accountants, Mutual Funds Sales and Marketing Representatives, Banking Support Services Analysts, Computer Systems Designers, Telemarketing Professionals, Insurance Sales and Claims Representatives, and New Accounts Processors."

I hate to complain,

"I would like to open an account."

"Certainly. Business or Personal?"

"It's for me."

"That would be personal ... savings or chequing?"

"Um ... savings."

"That will be Miss Simpson. Please take a seat and she will be with you shortly."

In just a little more than an hour, a lovely young lady approached me. She was nattily attired in a pair of jeans with the knees out and a beer shirt.

"I'm Miss Simpson. How may I help you ... Mr....?"

"Foster ... Jim."

"Do you have any identification, Mr. Foster?"

"I really don't need any. I know who I am."

"I'm sure you do, Mr. Foster. But I need your driver's licence and two more pieces of identification."

"Well I have a licence, the card that came with the wallet, and an organ donor card that says that my body should be sent to St. Mary's Finishing School for Girls, but only if I'm still alive."

"Very whimsical, Mr. Foster. I'll need two other pieces of identification. But I suppose we can get started and you can drop them in later. Would you like to be able to write cheques on this account, Mr. Foster?"

"I suppose I should. Are they free?"

"There is a small charge of $15.40, plus a little extra depending on the picture, but we can simply scoff that out of your account. Now you will need an ATM card to access your account. There is a modest charge for withdrawals. However at your advanced age, for only $9.50 per month you can make as many as five transactions a month at no charge. I do need a few bits of personal information, all confidential of course. You are employed, Mr. Foster?"

"Yes, I am a columnist at the *Packet*."

"That's very impressive. I imagine that must be a fairly lucrative profession."

"Yes."

"We have a special on our platinum Visa that can be used to pay off all your other cards. Plus it gives air miles and fifty cents off on a new Lincoln. Do you currently have any credit cards?"

"Well I had one until yesterday, but the man at the Liquor Store cut it in half."

but…

"I see. Just how much do you make, Mr. Foster?"
"Fifty dollars a month."
"Goodbye, Mr. Foster."

This was my very first column. A few people were upset. but we do have more than our share of wackos in Orillia.

This is not exactly Sanity City
November 4, 1995

I was in the Chamber of Commerce office the other day waiting to see Susan Lang, Ed Holcomb's replacement. (A hell of a lot cuter than Ed, by the way.)

While I was there, I started to browse through the brochures advertising Orillia, the Sunshine Town. As I read them, I started to think, "This is not the Orillia I know ... not by a long shot." You only have to hang around this burg a few weeks till it begins to dawn on you, that this is not exactly Sanity City.

I was talking to Clayt the other day and the more I looked at him, the more I realized how tired he was. And it has to be the result of being mayor of this nuthouse.

Did you know that Orillia is the only city in North America with more protest groups than citizens? No matter what idea is presented or passed at council, we can guarantee that within twenty minutes an organization will be formed to protest the idea, and within an hour, picketers will be marching around City Hall.

Under the provisions of the British North America Act, all protest groups in Orillia must be designated by a three — letter acronym beginning with C.A.— such as C.A.N... C.A.D... etc. Any normal citizen of course, knows that the whole damn bunch of them can be lumped under one four-lettered acronym, C.R.A.P.

On the morning of June 14, 1062, at a quarter to seven, an Ojibway brave, Running Bear Stinson, invented the birch bark canoe. At a quarter to eight, a Mrs. Pocohontas Cooney had scientific evidence that the chemical reaction of birch bark and Lake Couchiching water would surely contaminate the No. 2 well.

In 1618, Orillia was discovered by Samuel de Champlain, who landed at the foot of Mississaga Street. Not for food and water as was later documented by historians, but to try and find out who owned the scrap yard that was already leaking battery acid into the lake.

After narrowly escaping with his life in an encounter with the local branch of A.P.E.C., Sam took off for Barrie and hasn't been back since.

I'm sure you realize by now that this is not the most tolerant city in the world.

Now I don't know when they put up the statue of old Sammy in the park. I have to assume it was his birthday. But can you imagine the controversy if they tried to do it today?

A Frenchman? Mark my words: there would be bloodshed. Keith and Dick from A.P.E.C. would be firing up the crosses.

After Champlain left — as Harry Speed says, "to buy a used canoe from Paul Sadlon" they must have put a "closed for renovations" sign on the town dock because apparently nothing happened around here until 250 years later, when we were incorporated.

I guess I shouldn't be talking since I'm not a native Orillian. I've only been here for forty-five years. I went to public school in Toronto and never took any history of Orillia and Simcoe County. I suspect however that no one up here did either.

The average person's history of Orillia seemed to start the day that Stevie Leacock took up serious drinking over on Brewery Bay.

As I was telling a bunch of folks at the Highwayman Inn a couple of years ago, typical of the Canadian reaction to anyone who makes a success of his life, Orillia chose to ignore the fact that Leacock was probably the greatest historian and humorist of his day, and remembered only that the man enjoyed a drink.

Orillia, as you know, was one of the last communities in Ontario to vote "Wet."

If the Lord had chosen to turn the water into wine at a wedding in Orillia, instead of Canaan, He would have been thrown in the slammer and we would now be the largest Islamic community outside of Baghdad.

I seemed to have run out of space. More about that later.

Remind me to tell you some time of the strange mathematical phenomenon concerning the number of calls to the "Talk of the Town" column and the appearance of a full moon.

I had just suffered through another Saturday evening with Elwy.

When did those old greats stop being so great?
November 21, 1995

The humour of the radio shows and movies from a long time ago, was clean and it was funny.

Joannie Asselin is saying right now, "What does that little degenerate know about clean humour?" (Joannie is the same girl that brought her guacamole dip so often to Mariposa Arts Theatre parties, that whenever there was a potluck coming up, the guests automatically phoned the hospital and reserved the stomach pump.) But humour changes and so does a lot of things .

If you want to test that out, tune in to Elwy Yost on "Saturday Night at the Movies."

Old Elwy shows all the classic movies from the Thirties, or even farther back. He just goes nuts because they are so wonderful. Meanwhile, I'm sitting there thinking, "I loved that movie forty years ago. When did it become so stupid?"

Is there some kind of virus that sneaks into old movies and rewrites them? You don't have to go back that far either. If City-TV shows *The Ten Commandments* one more time, I'll turn Buddhist.

It isn't the story. I guess it's the acting ... or maybe a bit of both. Let's take a look at that classic for a moment. We have 40,000 people wandering around the desert for forty years, following some guy who doesn't know where he's going — like a Biblical Jacques Parizeau.

Don't you think that at some time, some one would have said, "Look Moses, this isn't a complaint or anything, but do you think I could take a peek at that map you've got up there? How about stopping at the next Esso station and asking the guy how to get to the Promised Land? I think we should have turned right at that fig tree twenty-seven years ago."

Actually, I think they should re-shoot that movie and recast it. Can't you see Jean Chretien as Moses, Mike Duffy as Pharaoh (same haircut), Sheila Copps as Mrs. Moses, and Preston Manning as the little weasel played by Edward G. Robinson?

I know I've been a little hard on Preston the last couple of weeks, but Squeaky Manning had the audacity to criticize Chretien for leaving Sheila in charge when he went to Yitzhak Rabin's funeral, because she would have an "extremely negative impact on both the House and the

Unity Issue." While during the referendum, everyone in the country was wishing Preston would just clam up before he lost the vote all by himself.

I guess I shouldn't pick on Preston. It isn't easy going through life with the voice of a cartoon mouse. (There go the Reform readers. Maybe not, most of them left for Florida in October.)

But back to Elwy. Don't you just love the little rascal to pieces? They must have some sort of incentive plan down there at TVO, that the person who comes up with the most boring program format gets exempt from watching Elwy Yost. Old Elwy is the only guy in Canada who gets so turned on by old movies that he has to wear Depends every Saturday night. I'm sure that his idea of a great sexual experience would be to lie naked on his bed while his wife shows him pictures of Cecil B. DeMille.

I must be getting old. I can't sit through the big blockbuster movies anymore. Even *Gone with the Wind* is too much for me.

Come to think of it, I never liked that movie. That scene where they are burning Atlanta scares me. It looks too much like the place I'm going to for making fun of TV evangelists.

Twenty years ago, they ran *Bridge on the River Kwai* on CTV with only one Ford commercial during the intermission. The commercial was so long that the Ford plant retooled right in the middle of it. By the time everyone got down to Thor Motors, all the cars on the lot were last year's model.

The TV channels could help out though by whipping out an hour and a half of commercials. I don't know why they do that. I was saying the same thing to my wife this morning, as I sat there in my Fruit of the Loom panties, L'Eggs Pantihose, and drinking Labatt's Blue Light by the half gallon.

I've always been a James Bond fan. The other night they showed the last Bond film that Sean Connery made. He made it about fifteen years after all his others. Instead of his Aston Martin, he was driving around in a motorized wheelchair. The movie didn't start until 11:30 at night and was supposed to run for three hours. I finally decided that even I couldn't wait up to see whether an eighty-year-old Bond could 'rassle some twenty-five-year-old bimbo without going into cardiac arrest. So I let it go and checked the obits in the morning.

I do run on and say so little — kind of like Dave Macdonald filling us in on the Fairgrieve situation. Dave is the Chairman of the Police Commission and Paul Fairgrieve is the Chief of Police and is in deep doodoo.

but...

Oops, that was a mistake. Never take a shot at the Parade Marshal of the Scottish Festival. Next July, there'll be twenty-five highland bands tromping through the wife's marigolds.

Gotta go. Montel Williams is coming on. Today the topic is "How to dress for a TV talk show," or "I didn't know you could buy sweatpants by the square mile."

There's nothing that adds to a fine movie like a bit of bare skin.

What's tragedy without nudity?
March 10, 1998

It's not often that a columnist in the *Packet* has to challenge the work of another. But every now and then it becomes necessary for me to chastise one of my colleagues. I could not accept Kate Grigg's criticism of the blockbuster movie *Titanic* without doing what I feel is the definitive review of the movie.

Kate is a fine person but I'm afraid that my opinion of a movie carries much more weight than hers because I am older and therefore wiser. I use much the same logic to say that I know far more about the travel business than Dave Shaw, far more about electricity than Ken McCann, far more about running a city than Ian Brown, because I am years older. It also explains why Pete McGarvey knows far more than almost everyone north of Toronto.

My review is based on over a half-century of movie-going and on experience in the back row of the Orillia Opera House, not on something as subjective as simply watching a movie.

I have no problem with Kate criticizing the movie's direction, the weak storyline, the over-use of special effects, even the musical score (trombones 6, violins 0), but to have the audacity to even suggest that the nude scene was not necessary to the plot was inexcusable. That was the only reason I went. How can anyone properly film one of the world's great tragedies without the obligatory nude scene?

There has yet to be a movie made that could not have been improved by a few clips of a starlet in her altogether. *Gone with the Wind* would have been a far better movie if the ladies had tugged on Scarlett's corset strings until she popped right out the top and showed us why Rhett was always hanging around the plantation. I suspect that she may have had some serious body flaws, otherwise Ashley Wilkes wouldn't have dumped her to marry Melanie, who seemed to be crying most of the time.

At the end of *Sleepless in Seattle*, wouldn't the touching scene at the end where Tom Hanks finally meets Meg Ryan have been far more romantic if a gust of wind had come up and blown her clothes off the top of the Empire State Building? I thought the director ruined that part.

Kate seems to have missed the very essence of the movie. No one went to see the boat sink. (Oops, I gave away the plot.) They went to see Kate Winslet stretched out on a couch wearing nothing but a jewel the size of an auk egg.

Granted, not all great film stars should be seen in the buff. I suspect that Charles Laughton standing naked in the fine film *Witness for the Prosecution* might have cut down the box office receipts by three or four billion. But the odd shot of Marlene Deitrich wouldn't have been all that bad ... although I think she was close to a hundred at the time.

I started to question Kate's values shortly after I met her. I told a particularly funny story and I noticed that Kate, Joella, and Sarah Papple got all flustered and ran next door to Timmy Hortons. Although now that I think about it, the story may have been a little questionable since Bruce MacIntyre, the publisher, quit that afternoon and moved to New Brunswick.

As much as I am one of Stevie Leacock's greatest fans, I think his Sunshine Sketches would have been a far more realistic and a much better book had Zena Pepperleigh and young Peter Pupkin spent a few more hours skinny dippin' in Pumpkin Bay and a little less time riding around town on a bicycle.

But I digress: *Titanic* was a fine movie, although I have to admit I missed part of it. During the opening credits, I told the lady sitting ahead of me to take off her ugly hat and she wasn't wearing one. Her husband, Bruno, took me outside and helped me to see the seriousness of my comment by taking a roll of quarters and pounding them with pneumatic regularity on the end of my nose. By the time I got back in, Kate Winslet was just stretching out on the sofa. I stood up to get a better view and spilled a half-litre of coke on Mrs. Bruno. When I regained consciousness I was alone in the theatre and covered in footprints and popcorn kernels. But I liked the movie, at least the part I saw.

Did I mention Kate Winslet was barenaked?

When you are old, you remember all this stuff.

I used to feed on serials
November 26, 1996

The other day, I was reading an article on the greatest movies of all time. There was the usual line-up — *Citizen Kane ... It's a Wonderful Life ... Ace Ventura, Pet Detective* — all chosen by a panel of distinguished movie critics. (A distinguished critic is someone who gets in for nothing and therefore can afford to see all these classics.)

But for some reason, nobody picked, "the serials."

In the Fifties they had serials every Saturday afternoon at the old Oxford Theatre on the Danforth. All my heroes were there: Mandrake the Magician, Flash Gordon, and my all-time favourite, The Phantom.

The Phantom wore long grey underwear that went from his toes to the top of his head. (Maybe they started out white and ended up grey, we didn't have New Ultra Tide back then.) I can't remember if he had a trapdoor in the back.

The Phantom wore a mask that he borrowed from the Lone Ranger ... as if somebody would care who a guy was with his nose sticking out of a pair of Stanfields. I can't remember what he did for a living, but I know he wasn't doing all that well with the ladies. In the Fifties if a guy showed up at a girl's door wearing a full-length body stocking and a mask, she'd shove him down the front steps. Nowadays, she'd just assume he was wearing something by Alfred Sung.

The serials were my life when I was a kid. The hero was always up to his bum in alligators just as the picture ended. You had to wait all week to see how he got out of, or out from under, whatever mess he was in the week before.

Quicksand was good stuff. When you left, the Phantom would be in up to his neck and sinking like a rock. You knew he was only ten seconds away from being next week's headlines in the obit's.

When you came back a week later, he was only in to his ankles, and while we were away, a tree had suddenly grown up and a branch as the size of Marlon Brando was now hanging over his head. Plus he had a ladder, fifty feet of rope, and a grappling hook.

Just as you were starting to think he was finally safe, the poor slob got caught in an avalanche and you knew for sure that this time he'd really bought the farm. So you had to go home and sweat out another week. Which was good, because it gave the crew time to change the avalanche to a bookshelf and when you came back he was buried under the complete works of Mickey Spillane.

The best thing about serials was they were completely interchangeable. They'd shoot the Phantom caught in a man-eating plant, haul him out and stick in Jungle Jim or Sabu, the Elephant Boy. It didn't matter: the plot was all the same.

Man-eating plants were all the rage in the serials. They probably ate a half a dozen natives a week back then. Sometimes they'd have a white guy for dessert, but usually they were reserved for the giant spiders.

This was all Saturday afternoon matinee stuff ... five hundred kids screaming and throwing popcorn boxes. Whenever there was a spook show, the john was jammed with little nippers waiting until the scary part was over. I remember when Abbott and Costello met Frankenstein, there was so many kids in the can that the only place left to pee was some other guy's pocket.

There wasn't much sex in the serials. For one thing, the whole audience was eight or nine years old. Kissing a girl would cause a riot, and pulling the heroine's top down would be completely unacceptable.

The Bowery Boys were big in the Forties and early Fifties, but they were on their way out. For one thing, the "boys" were all fifty years old, and just didn't look right running around in a haunted house wearing pork-pie hats.

There was no sex at all in the Bowery Boys. There was always a dude named Gabe who was older and wore a suit. Every picture he was just about to get married. The last I time I saw Gabe was in 1988 and he still hadn't made it to the altar. If the rest of the gang ever had a relationship with a girl, it would have just been someone to whack with his hat.

My dad took me to a matinee (once) after he came back from the war. I was such a jerk, on the way home he dropped off at the Armouries and tried to re-enlist.

But finally you outgrew the matinees. You realized that it was time to set aside your childish fantasies and look for quality entertainment ... like swashbuckling with Errol Flynn, or *Indian-shootin' with John Wayne.

*Nowadays if you go looking for Indian-shootin', you've got yourself a trip before a Human Rights Tribunal and your chances of winning any money at the Rama Casino are practically non-existent.

This was one of the rare columns that my editor chopped up. Jeff didn't like me mentioning the rival rag.

An evening of gastronomical delights
November 28, 1995

There's an ad in the "Sincerely Yours" column of *Orillia Today* this week, about a couple in their sixties looking for another couple to fulfill their fantasies. Now I don't suppose I have much of a problem with that really — but 60? Wouldn't you think it would get kind of confusing with all those IV bottles and tubes hanging around? I better call John Mundell and Bob Carson, the local undertakers, to see if they have a room for four.

***

The other day I decided to tackle the monumental task of cleaning our basement. Not that it needed it all that much, but my neighbour happened to mention something about his basement floor and I couldn't remember if we had one. Right on top of a pile of magazines that I have been saving until I could figure out if I could put them in the blue box, I found a copy of *Toronto Life* from a few years ago. I'm not sure what year, but Louis St. Laurent's picture was on the cover.

The magazine was the Christmas edition ... about forty pounds of high gloss paper and stapled inside was a supplement called *Epicure* — sort of a Playboy centrefold for the glutton.

Now *Epicure* is a rather fascinating magazine because it pushes things that you and I will never eat, and restaurants where you and I will never go.

Now I have to admit that I have never tried any of the recipes in *Epicure*. But I have some reservation about trying anything that calls for saltpetre.

But the restaurants ... Now we've all read reviews in the *Toronto Star*, never the *Packet*. The *Packet*'s idea of fine dining is the Dickie Dee Wagon. (Except you can't buy it in Orillia because the City Council was afraid that a bunch of kids selling ice cream from a bicycle would destroy the economic stability of Orillia.)

But you know how it works. The reviewer (who must be the size of Marlon Brando by now — just slightly larger than the Village of

Coldwater) picks up some chick and off they go ... unannounced, to one of the local beaneries.

The waiter, who doesn't have a clue who this guy is, sits them down by the kitchen door.

Incidentally guys, it is considered very low class for the ladies to have to sit by the kitchen door. So if you are dining out with the girl of your dreams — or even your wife — you should never accept these seats. In spite of the fact that it is probably the only seats in the restaurant close enough to the stove so your soup doesn't have icebergs floating in it.

Now at the end of this little review is the average price of dinner for two, plus a bottle of the local house bingo.

An example (actual review):

NEKAH..cooly spiritual throughout, with two daily Prix Fixe of minimalist tones (the bias seafood and game, the provenance significantly Canadian, matched wines) it requires an evening.

A White Salmon Fillet shimmers beneath the surface of intensely flavoured Grouper Consomme.. Rare-Grilled Tuna is threaded on Lemongrass..Roasted Buffalo leg sauced by Redcurrants...Petit Fours rest on a rock slab strewn with Pansy Petals..(edible). A La Carte as well..$130 – $200.

Licensed –32 Wellington Street. Major credit cards accepted.*

Do you see what I mean? A whole magazine full of this stuff. Two hundred bucks! What if you blew two hundred bucks on her and when you get her home she has a headache?

Wouldn't it be a lot better to hustle her off to French's Stand and buy her a hot dog? Then if she has a headache, you can always head down to the Legion and drink beer until the bartender turns out the lights. (Now students, that's sexist. But don't bother to call, my wife is going to kill me anyway.)

But can't you see a review in *Epicure* for that evening?

Le Stand du Frenchman.. on the shores of beautiful Lac Couchiching.. a quaint little open-air Cafe.. jackets suggested after November..nicely appointed..Twin Pailles du Garbage.. Strategically situated, so the more athletic diner may practise hook shots with a napkin..should he or she choose to use one.

but...

Milady ordered Le Chien Chaud avec une Order de Side
Patates Frits. Le Chien Chaud was placed lovingly dans une
bunne nestled dans une sleeve cardboard.. the Patates Frit,
still dripping, and salted ever so lightly as to cause cardiac
arrest in a Yak.. were dumped in une bag papier.

Monsieur, suffering from an evening of merriment,
ordered deux Rolaid dans une bed du bread dry.

A delightful little house wine.. Chez Mountain Dew,
complemented dinner.

The evening's entertainment was supplied by the occasional
wasp and the unexpected arrival of the Central Ontario Chapter
of Hell's Angel who delighted one and all with the savage
beating of a park attendent.

$5.00–$10.00 ..no credit cards accepted... Shoes optional.

An interesting observation: Nekah appears to have gone out of
business ... at least they are no longer in the Toronto phone book. Le
Stand du Frenchman, however, was here when Sammy Champlain
was around, and is still here today.

(I had trouble with the French menu since I was given 50 in
Grade 11, on condition that I didn't show up for French in Grade 12.)

* Review reprinted with the permission of *Toronto Life*.

I fear this column needs no explanation.

LISTEN UP, THIS IS SERIOUS STUFF
December 26, 1995

I had originally planned on writing a column about Christmas, an epistle filled with the tales of joy and gladness of the holiday season. But circumstances change and an unfortunate peek at myself in a full-length mirror forced me to deal with a subject that cries out for public examination — the perfection of the human body.

One of the problems we face in our society is that we have a very unrealistic idea of what the perfect specimen of our species should be. Because of the influence of the advertising media and the way we almost worship movie and sport personalities, we have a mindset of what the "beautiful" people should look like.

Women should look like Loni Anderson and men should look like my friend, Bill Price, or Wayne Gretzky.

This is not only unrealistic but probably mentally and physically unhealthy. We are simply not all capable of reaching this perfection of the physical form.

But we owe it to ourselves, our lovers, and yes, even to our spouses to at least try and reach some level of physical fitness. Therefore it behooves me ... (I love the word "behooves." I have no idea what it means, unfortunately) ... It behooves me to do a series of articles on our bodies.

A brief history of our quest for physical beauty:

Since very few members of our community (with the possible exception of a few of the senior members of council) can remember what a caveman looked like, I thought I would start our investigation with the Ancient Greeks. I'm not talking about Dean Heliotis here, but further back to the days of Athens and Sparta, at the original Olympics.

As anyone who has studied Greek sculpture can see this was the beginning of true physical beauty. Although it appears that the women didn't have any arms back then, which left them fairly helpless at the drive-in.

The reason it was so important to develop the perfect athletic form was not to enhance their performance in a particular event, but because in the original games they all ran around barenaked. It is one thing to carry around a couple of extra pounds when you can wear a pair of baggy sweatpants. It is quite another to display your love handles and cellulited thighs to an arena full of spectators.

However, that period in history was a fleeting moment before the Romans started us on the rapid road to obesity. Granted, the Roman Legions were probably excellent specimens of fitness. Well you would be too, marching all over the countryside raping and pillaging ... whatever pillaging means. Probably the same as behooving.

But the aristocracy was a far cry from the Legions. Their only exercise was to roll over and grab a handful of grapes and another flagon of wine. Over a century or so, they managed to get so far out of shape that they had to invent the toga to cover up the accumulated blubber from a hundred years of "porcus maximus" (Latin for pigging-out).

And so over the centuries the human body became what it is today, a far cry from the Olympic athlete, with the exception of course of Loni Anderson and Bill Price.

Since none of us are serious enough about it to actually want to exercise or anything strenuous like that, we must, I hesitate to mention it, yes, we must diet.

But how to we go about that? Which diet do we use? I have, in the interest of the community, tried a number of the more popular ones.

In 1985, the big rage was the Drinking Man's Diet based on the idea that you could drink all you wanted and the alcohol would eat up all the fat calories. Never mind why they should be able to do that; only a few of us are bright enough to understand. But I threw myself into the Drinking Man's Diet to such an extent in '85, that I can't remember '86, or '87, and woke up somewhere in '89, wandering naked in a strange city, wearing a pinwheel hat.

Not discouraged, I tried Dr. Stillman's Water Diet, which consisted of all the hard-boiled eggs you could eat and enough water every day to float the *Island Princess*. The old Doc was on Johnny Carson one night and said that all the cholesterol in his diet wouldn't do half as much damage to your heart as lugging around all the fat. A week later, Stillman was dead. I have no idea what killed him, but I understand he was buried in an egg crate.

Next I tried the Stewardess's Diet, which was one of the first "Chemical" diets. You only had to stay on it four days then you could eat an ox on the weekend. I tried it for a month, but quit when I realized that I hadn't lost a pound and had started wearing women's underwear

but...

and hanging around the Pilots' Lounge at Toronto International Airport.

Unfortunately I have to stop here. Jeff Day, the editor, won't give me any more space. Of course he's skinny and doesn't understand the seriousness of the problem.

Stay tuned, next week I'll tell you how to perform your own liposuction with a vacuum cleaner and fifty feet of garden hose.

Still fat.

On a roll ... around the middle
January 2, 1996

Well here we are two days into another year and anxious to continue down the road to physical fitness.

If you remember, I was going to tell you about the home liposuction program. A slight problem has arisen. It appears that improper manipulation of your Electrolux may cause Popeye Syndrome, which is pipe cleaner arms and wrists the size of tree stumps.

One of the big problems of diets is trying to determine what you should weigh in the first place. For years doctors were using the Metropolitan Life Weight Charts as some sort of guide as to what their patients should weigh. You know the one I mean, it was based on your sex, if any, your height, and whether or not you were big or small boned. Short of taking out one of your leg bones and measuring it, how were you supposed to know whether you were big-boned or not?

I used to work with Walter Henry, an Olympic boxer. Walter and I are the same height. At one time I weighed 195 pounds. I looked like Dom Deluise after a spaghetti binge. Since I could no longer get in and out of a chair without one of Knight's cranes, I went on a diet. Walter said "Are you losing weight?" and I said, "As a matter of fact, thirty-five pounds." Walter said "I've put on a couple. When I was boxing I weighed 124 lbs, but I've ballooned up to 126." So I said "Oh yeah, but I'm big-boned."

I'm still too heavy, but my big problem right now is how to mask this roll around my middle.

I had this friend in school who put on so much weight one summer that he could stop an escalator. He said that his pot was not caused by fat at all, but was overdeveloped stomach muscles caused by slugging around milk cans in a dairy all summer. And he may have been right. I have seen pictures of Elsie the Cow and she was built exactly the same way he was.

We have to be careful here, that we don't try to hide our physical failures by trying to disguise them. I tried wearing an old refrigerator shipping crate that I borrowed from Foster Appliances, but one Thursday I wandered too close to the road and was picked up in the Blue Box program.

Another popular way of disguising your extra poundage is to wear vertical stripes. The idea of course is that vertical stripes make you appear thinner. What it actually does, I'm afraid, is create the illusion that you are wearing that yellow striped beer tent they use at the Scottish Festival.

Public sunbathing is, of course, out of the question. The only way I would dare go to Moose Beach in the summer is to arrive at 7:00 in the morning and hire two kids to cover me with sand.

I'm afraid, my friends, that we must face the fact that if we are going to go out in public, at least in the daylight, we must lose weight.

Shortly after my heart blocked up like a Dairy Queen Blizzard in a straw, Dr. Bhatt sent me off to the Pain House to a seminar on healthy eating. Deven was worried about my cholesterol readings. I wasn't. I was worried about my triglycerides. If they are high you have to stop drinking beer.

I must admit that most of their information was interesting, but I slipped out to get a bag of chips and by the time I got back the seminar was over. I won't go back. If they don't care enough about their patients to have snackies, then I don't care enough to go.

I started to seriously think about actually doing some exercises but most of them seem to require bending over and stuff like that. I would think that that sort of thing could be fatal to a person my age.

There was an excellent article in October's *Gentlemen's Quarterly*, on working out with dumbbells. But I do that every April with the cast of *Oh Really Orillia* and wouldn't want to do it on a regular basis. (I didn't realize until I checked the dictionary that dumbbell had two "b"s in it. Which suggests that I might be one myself.)

But I think that the exercise route is the only way to go. I wouldn't feel right recommending that you readers try any of this stuff without going through the program myself.

So just a few minutes ago I started with dumbbell exercise number one, "The Squat."

It says, "holding the dumbbells at your sides, slowly sink into a crouch." Well, I'm down here but for some reason I don't seem to be able to get back up. Sharon won't be home until five o'clock. I wonder if I can waddle over as far as the television set.

If anyone can think of any other way I can get back in shape, drop by and tell me. Oh yeah — bring a bag of chips.

It's over. That's it. I have a cold.
January 9, 1996

In spite of my magnificent physical condition, developed by years of exercise and healthy living, I doubt that I will live much past noon hour. I have a cold.

Oh please don't send get-well cards and those little Biblical messages. By the time Mr. Gardiner, my mail person, gets here I'll be pretty well toast. A taxi with a load of Johnny Walker's Sipping Medicine might make it in time, but you'll have to hurry.

I've tried everything ... straight scotch, rye and hot water, cold beer, warm beer. Lisa from the Wine Store sent down an emergency jug of Bright's House, but it's no use. I'm gone.

I'm so desperate, I even tried watching the Vision Channel to see if my old buddy Swaggart might be doing a faith-healing session. But it was Sunday morning and all I could get was The Zoroastrian Concert Band playing the theme song from *Aladdin* on a zither.

It's not that I'm all that afraid of going, it's just that I'll never know if Lucien Bouchard is really the reincarnation of Charles DeGaulle or not.

I'll have no friends up there. On the bright side though, there won't be any lawyers. But it's you people I worry about. Here I've got you started on the road to fitness, and me, your guru of physical perfection, is about to be taken from you.

The signs are all there. My faculties are breaking down. Yesterday I watched the Geraldo Rivera Show and I thought I saw a guest in a suit. You know Geraldo. He's the guy who on his own show in 1992 had fat removed from his buttocks and injected into his forehead, which may say all the needs to be said about American TV.

I even phoned my sister. Maureen's a nurse who, much to the horror of my folks, took off to Winnipeg in 1961 where she revolutionized the medical profession by actually warming the bedpans before shoving them under the shivering bottoms of the sick. The savings to Manitoba in lock de-icer alone must have run into the millions.

I have great respect for her medical knowledge. She trained at East General in Toronto in the Fifties. She was going to nurse here, but OSMH was still big on leeches back then. As a matter of interest, I've heard that with Big Al McLean and Mike Harris cutting back on their support payments, Glen Penwarden, the Administrator, and John Mueller, the Chief of Staff, have been seen turning over rocks in Silver Creek every afternoon.

But Maureen was no help. She had been cleaning the attic and caught a cold from my picture in the 1953 Oricolle yearbook.

I was afraid to call my mother. She's into a kind of folk medicine based on getting out of bed and actually doing something. Or "if it's that bad, go to the doctor." Which is a little unrealistic, if you ask me.

My wife has it too. At least I think it's her. There is a big lump under the covers, and every ten minutes an arm comes up and throws a handful of Kleenex in the general vicinity of the wastepaper basket. However she went to work. Which is understandable. Women don't feel pain the way men do. After all, they are not that far up the evolutionary scale. But they are getting there and already can be trained to do certain household tasks. In the meantime, I'm lying here suffering alone.

I phoned the neighbours but they weren't all that interested in my symptoms. (Although Hughie next door said to tell Sharon that he'd cut the lawn for her when I'm gone.)

While I was writing this, through my tears I found a flyer that we got just before Christmas, advertising a book called "Doctors' ASTOUNDING Secret Cures" and I think I'll send away for it. If I'm still alive by the time it gets here, I'll bet there's a cure in there.

Actually I'm quite excited about this book. Apparently there are some amazing remedies: how to cure dandruff by pouring hot olive oil on your head, or a cure for aging hair by rubbing thirty-two cents worth of mayonnaise on your noggin. Here's a good one, a cure for hemorrhoids using twelve cents worth of apple sauce. I don't think I want to know how you get the apple sauce in there.

I only hope I last long enough to try some of this stuff. Wait a minute. A taxi just pulled in the laneway.

"A whole case? Oh bless you, sir. Bless you."

In Orillia, we are allowed to write about sex, although none of us understand it.

Yup, it's that sex thing again
November 11, 1997

Recently I read two articles in the *Packet* that dealt with, dare I say it ... sexual matters. That suggests to me, that Mark Bisset, the news editor, has somehow tapped into the *Playboy* website, or someone has been slipping weird chemicals into the water. (There is no coffee machine in the newsroom at the *Packet*. I only mention that so you will understand that their weird political views are coming from minds totally freaked out by caffeine deprivation.)

A couple of weeks ago on the Canada and the World page, I learned that sex changes part of a rat's brain. I never knew that. I thought they ran up and down stairs all night because of a chemical reaction to cheddar cheese. The researcher, who obviously must have sexual interests that would shock Marv Albert, announced this revelation as if it was the greatest discovery since King Arthur found Lancelot's teeth in Guinevere's underwear drawer.

Marc Breedlove, a Professor of Psychology at Berkeley, (with a name like Breedlove, you know he wouldn't be in a sane occupation) said that he found structural changes in the rat's brain and at the base of its spinal cord. I must admit that I was fascinated ... oh not by his conclusions, but that a man could actually make a living prying into the sex life of rodents. How does a man become interested in a thing like that? I hate to even suggest it, but could it be the fault of Walt Disney? Did little Marc spend far too many hours wondering what was under Minnie's polka-dot mini-skirt? I thought I was a little strange because I got excited watching the Phantom run around in a purple union suit.

That article was in mid-October. Then on the same page two weeks later, I learned that people around the world are having more sex. Apparently the French seem to have quite an interest in it ... they frolic 151 times a year, or say they do, the Americans, 148. (the article didn't say where we were, probably too embarrassed.) The French also bumped us Canadians out of first place as the most considerate lovers. That's really bad news. We all thought we were pretty good, and now we can't even win Miss Congeniality.

I have nothing against polls, although I wouldn't believe a thing they came up with. For instance, some still suggest that Mike Harris is a popular premier. (Actually I hope they interviewed Mike in this latest sex poll. He should be an expert after what he's been doing to the Province for two straight years.)

I have never been able to understand why people would answer questions about their sex life. How accurate do you really think a poll is about the shenanigans going on behind someone's bedroom door? If some yo-yo started prying into your love life, how honest are you really going to be? Don't you think that most folks would be inclined to stretch the truth just a little? If someone knocked on your door and asked you when was the last time you fiddled around in the marriage bed, even if the last time was on V-J Day, wouldn't you be inclined to say, "Last night, and again this morning"?

The survey found that Italians gallop through sex, taking only 13.8 minutes before going back to listening to the opera, or painting chapel ceilings, whatever Italians do in their spare time. Americans have the most stamina and keep going for almost a half an hour. My friends, be honest. Have you ever met an American who could tear himself away from a football game long enough to shake her hand, let alone blow a whole half an hour in the bedroom? His missus doesn't have the time either, she has to get down to her aerobics class. "Will you be much longer, dear? Our class has a Richard Simmons video today. By the way, the ceiling needs painting. Do you know any Italians?"

What I did find fascinating (this wasn't in the *Packet*, I heard it on the CBC), Canadians find the Polish people the most undesirable lovers, and by a strange coincidence, the Poles find us equally as unappetizing. I have no idea why this should be so, but it does explain why I have never had fantasies of being alone with Lech Walesa.

I suppose that all these polls have some useful purpose, other than giving jobs to people with an unhealthy interest in someone else's bedroom, but I would want to see a list of the people they interviewed. For instance, it would be ridiculous if senior citizens and young newlywed couples were included in the same statistics. The newlyweds have to get up for work, while the seniors can fool around all day.

I'm thinking of starting my own sex poll. Not that I would ever publish the results: I'm just kind of nosy.

This is part of a series I'm going to write some day for the young folks.

The art of love: it's all in the arms
March 3, 1998

A year ago I wrote a fine column on dating that is now a teaching guide in the more progressive schools in Canada and the United States. As my contribution to the mental health of the modern teenager, I have decided to write a series for boys as they start down the road to romantic bliss.

It helps to find a girl. Short of running an ad in the *Packet*, it makes a little more sense to ask a girl in your class. On second thought, ask a girl roughly your age in another class. That way if you totally screw up, you won't have to sit there while she smirks and all the other girls giggle like you are Gomer Pyle.

The best way to choose a young lady for an evening of passion is to list all of the available candidates. Usually the list would start with the girl of your dreams. (Not THOSE dreams: there are no women like that — at least not outside a mental institution.) If there is one fair lady you would like to be stranded with on an island, put her at the top of the list.

Write her name everywhere — on your notes, textbooks, your intimate athletic equipment, or carved into your desk. Practise writing her name as Mrs. Algernon Eggplant, or whatever your name is, until the kid beside you notices it scrawled all over and tells the rest of the school. Immediately transfer to another class, if possible in Bolivia.

Continue until you have all the young damsels jotted down in order of desirability. START AT THE BOTTOM. This may explain why the best-looking girl in the school has no dates whatsoever and ends up at the formal with her older brother, or the class nerd. Every boy in the school worships her but is afraid to ask her out for fear of an embarrassing refusal. If the truth were known she'd accept a date with a goat if he'd ask.

The theatre, when I was a teenager was a training ground for serious romance. It was here that you practised the basic finger twine, the more advanced around the shoulder arm sneak, and many other necessary manoeuvres that would be your stock in trade until you got married and forgot everything you ever learned.

There is an art to putting your arm around a girl in a theatre. Depending on the time of year, it can be simple, or an exercise requiring as much pre-planning and strategy as the raid on the Guns of Navarone.

In the winter, you simply reach around her shoulder to help her with her coat and leave your arm there. That is the "around the shoulder arm sneak" and can be done by almost anyone. If you don't think you can quite master it without diagrams, it is covered extensively in the Kama Sutra — but unfortunately in Sanskrit.

The summertime shoulder sneak is complex and has to be handled with great care and finesse. For one thing, all a girl needs when it's 95 degrees is some yo-yo's sweaty arm draped over her shoulder. (Incidently, a course on basic hygiene and a field trip to a deodorant counter is a prerequisite here.) The simplest and most common manoeuvre, of course, is the arm stretch. The gentleman fakes a yawn and sticks his arm straight in the air, saying casually, "Ho Hum," gently lowering his arm across the back of her seat — being careful not to whack her on the head.

Unfortunately, this is the most common move in a boys arsenal and murmurs of "he's making his move" will be whispered for three or four rows behind him. After a suitable period of inactivity, the hand will move ever so slightly towards her shoulder ... assuming it hasn't gone to sleep and has to be brought back for a pounding to get the blood moving. Finally your whole arm will be moved forward and draped casually across her shoulders. About that time, she will excuse herself to go to the washroom. When she comes back, if she comes back, you are in the awkward situation of having to repeat the process. I recommend waving like a madman to an imaginary friend, calling out "Harry" and dropping your arm on her shoulder again. If she immediately leaves for the john, you are faced with one of two possibilities: you are either dating a girl with a kidney infection, or you've struck out. Unless she's wearing Depends, I suspect the latter.

What it really comes down to is: taking a girl to the local bijou to make out is as bright as taking her to a biker bar to teach her the art of fine dining. Take her to a drive-in, that's what they are there for.

Next week: "Drive-in Etiquette" or "Don't look now but there's a cop looking through the back window."

The passion pit memoirs
May 31, 1998

Last week I promised a class on drive-in romance. I forgot the one in Orillia closed down years ago and the kids will have no idea what I'm talking about.

The drive-in theatre of the Fifties and Sixties was the research lab of the School of Romance. It was here that the techniques you heard in the boys locker room could be practised without prying eyes.

The drive-in was to the world of the theatre, what the Victory Burlesque was to the St. Mary's Finishing School for Young Ladies. Once a young girl went to the passion pit, as it was called in the vernacular of the day, it was assumed by her parents that she was on her way to motherhood or certain death, preferably the latter.

The drive-in was a world of its own. It was a place where couples could take the kids to play on the swings, or watch the swingers at play, whatever was their bag. It was also, I'm afraid, a mobile saloon.

A friend of mine had a 1927 Chev. I will not mention his name here. His wife, Jane Branch, may not want to hear of his shady past. When he got it, the Chev had just seven thousand miles on it. Thanks to a careful maintenance program and meticulous care, it never made eight. The '27 had a well under the back seat that would hold eighteen beers and a load of ice. It always amazed me that the design engineers at GM could foresee the need for such a reservoir twenty years before the invention of the drive-in itself.

It also had a trunk, but not like our modern versions: the trunk on the '27 was a metal box nailed over the rear bumper. One evening the O.P.P. were checking cars looking for beer. (Grass in the Fifties was the stuff your father made you mow every Saturday.) When they got to the '27, the officer asked if he could look in the trunk. The driver, my friend Da— Branch, said "certainly," and off they went to look at the wrenches and pop bottles in the trunk.

—ve proceeded to thank the officer for his diligence in protecting the morals of Canada's young people, and expressed his dismay that some chaps would drink in illegal places or while underaged, thereby besmirching the reputation of cleaner-cut young gentlemen like ourselves. In the world of B.S. it ranks up there with Bill and Monica's working late story.

The officer thanked us for our co-operation and let us through. He knew we had it somewhere, but probably figured anyone who would feed a cop a line like that deserved a beer.

Every now and then, a restricted movie would show up. Remember this was a restricted movie in the Fifties when married couples in the films had to sleep with one foot on the floor. Some of the stuff that we had to be 18 to watch is on Walt Disney today. There was a story going around that a young couple were refused admittance one evening because they had a six-month old baby in the car and the sign said "No Admittance Under Eighteen." I believe it. Censorship at a drive-in was like wearing a plunging neckline to a nudist camp. It made no sense at all. No matter what was going on up on the screen, there was far worse happening in a hundred back seats.

The biggest problem for romance at a drive-in was most of the time there were four people in the car. Girls usually preferred double dating. It's one thing smooching when you were alone, it's quite another knowing Fred and Ethel were peeking at you over the back seat.

None of the Big Three auto-makers cared enough for their fellow man to put any amount of research into the greatest problem of watching movies in the great outdoors, foggy windows. You could always judge how far a couple were along the path to bliss by the amount of steam on the windows. It usually cost $2.50 a carload to get in and $35.00 for gas to keep the windows clear. They could never have shown *The Ten Commandments* at a drive-in. The Israelites would have thought the Promised Land was downtown Come By Chance during a pea-souper and kept on going.

As I think back, if you weren't clearing the fog off the windows, you were whacking mosquitoes. If you weren't whacking mosquitoes, you were blowing your horn at some jerk who turned his lights on and washed out the picture. If you weren't blowing your horn, you were starting the car to get some heat. The more I look back, the more I realize that drive-ins were a disaster.

But more important, they are not good for the morals of our youth. I think they should be closed down across the country ... at least until all our grandchildren are married.

I love giving advice. Although I'm not great on taking it.

Sound advice from Mr. Foster
May 5, 1996

Dear Mr. Foster:

I am a young man of 35 living at home with my parents. I have been quite content with my lot in life until just recently, when I read an article in the *Packet* that referred to something called "girls." I believe that they are the ones my father has been talking to me about. Would it be a good idea for me to approach one or should I wait a few years?

Persival Persimmons

Dear Percy:

You seem a little young yet, but I've heard of young chaps that went out with women when they were in their late twenties, although their inexperience was painfully obvious and the girls quickly left them and found a more mature man in his late fifties. But you could try to engage one of these fascinating creatures in conversation. However I must warn you, they will very quickly swing the subject around to marriage and I think that you are much too young to consider such a step. Marriage is something that requires a lot of thought and I'm not sure that a youth of 35 is capable of making that decision. Some night, when your mommy is tucking you in and reading you your story, you might ask her to advise you on the pleasures of marriage and why she drinks gin all day.

First though, Percival, you have to actually meet a nice girl and that isn't the easiest thing to do. I know a whole bunch of older gentlemen from the Golden K Club, whose wives get sick of having them around the house and kick them out every Tuesday morning. These chaps have had all kinds of experience with women (women are just like girls except they are brighter and don't giggle as much).

I asked them the other day what lines they use to pick up women and they have several good ones. "Twenty-three skidoo" seems to be popular, "I love my wife, but, oh, you kid" runs a close second.

I would try standing out in front of the United Cigar store at nine o' clock on a Saturday night. Whenever a young girl walks by with her mother, you could jump out and shout either one of these surefire lines. If she's not interested, you might have a chance with her mother.

Let me know how you make out.

Mr. Foster

Dear Mr. Foster,

I tried your lines out last weekend and they didn't seem to work all that well. Perhaps I didn't say them properly. I think though, jumping out of a darkened doorway and shouting
"Twenty-three skidoo" was not a particularly good idea. Both the mother and the daughter wet their pants and took off up the street.

Percy

Dear Percy,

That's odd. I called the boys at the Golden K and told them what happened. Then they remembered, when they used to do it, the Salvation Army was playing hymns in front of the T.D. Bank and if she seemed interested, they could always ask her to dance.

By the way, you weren't naked at the time I hope? That doesn't always go over too well. I have a friend who tried that and got arrested. Plus, it was January and the freezing didn't come out until the 24th of May.

Have you tried joining a church group? Although that can be a problem. A friend of mine joined a Singles Club at St. Paul's and met a nice young lady who took him over to meet the minister. She then had him sign what he thought was a pledge sheet for the Cancer Society, and when he woke up in the morning, he was married with six kids. Then she made him babysit while she went off with the girls to play bingo and buy Nevada tickets all day.

The last I heard, she had won the jackpot and ran off with a beer salesman. He's stuck at home with six kids and he doesn't even know their names yet.

Other than that, I don't know what else you can do.

Mr. Foster

but…

Dear Mr. Foster:

I think my problem is solved. I've just been talking to a young girl from Hollywood, Elizabeth Taylor, who I think has been married before. She was down to the "P's" in the phone book and gave me a call.

I just have a couple of questions. Why should I eat lots of oysters? And, do you think she will read me my story ?

Percy

Something for the ladies.

Pretty slim pickings out there, Linda
May 12, 1996

Dear Mr. Foster

I was most impressed with your advice to teenaged boys on asking a young woman out on a date. However I am a spinster of some twenty-two summers and as you might expect am getting somewhat anxious. Do you think that I could use the same approach to snare a man ?

Linda Lust

Dear Linda,

Unfortunately, I seem to have lost my copy of last week's column and cannot afford to go out and actually buy a *Packet*. But off the top of my head, I would say definitely, no ... especially calling a man, you little tramp. I can understand your anxiety over your marital status. Once a girl reaches your advanced age, the chances of catching a first class man are practically nil. But miracles do happen, so don't give up hope.

Look at Madonna. Come to think of it, she's decided to go it alone, so she wasn't that great an example.

There are several things that you can try to attract a suitable man. You notice, I said, "suitable." There are lots of men out there, but not all are good husband material. For instance, what if you were to catch a hockey player? Most burn themselves out by the time they are 30, and have to be discarded in the Blue Box program. The ones that live have so few teeth left that their poor wives have to puree everything. There's nothing quite like a bowl full of steak.

My sister married late in life — she was almost 24 — but she had an unfair advantage. She was a nurse and when her husband Jack came out from under the ether, she was waiting with the preacher. He didn't even know her. (I was going to say anesthetic, but it didn't look right. I looked it up in two dictionaries and they are both wrong.)

You could try running an ad on the internet. The only problem with that is he will spend every working moment surfing the net and the only chance you will have to consummate the marriage is during a power break. I have a friend who had to have a mouse installed before he would pay any attention to her at all.

A number of girls have been successful by standing on the corner wearing a sweater with "easy" across the back. That does narrow the field somewhat, since the person you attract would have to be able to read, which pretty well rules out politicians and reporters.

I think that it is very important to dress well when you are out man-hunting. I find that fishnet stockings turn me on (of course so do fish, so I wouldn't go by that). Tight red sweaters are a must, unless you are built along the lines of a stickperson, then something loose would be more in order. I don't know whether minis are still in, but whatever skirt you wear, don't ever ever wear those little black boots. Nothing looks dumber than nice long legs and a pair of boots. I realize that's the style, but unless you are planning a career in the military, I'd give it a miss.

Have you considered a tattoo? I was in a line at Zellers last summer and the girl ahead of me had on a halter and peeking over the top was a tattoo of what might have been a flower or a tiger's head. I have to admit that I was completely mesmerized by the whole thing. I was hoping she would sneeze or something just so I could see what the rest of it was. I have always been intrigued by a girl with a tattoo. What if she should marry the governor general? Try to picture her being presented to the Queen, with "Property of Hell's Angels" peeking over the top her Giorgio Armani dress. She also had thirty or forty rings hanging from her ears and what appeared to be the Hope diamond in her nose. That is very big along the Zambesi.

Have you tried running an ad in the back of the *Packet*? Some guys have found the girl of their dreams in the back of a newspaper. Although, she usually costs $4.50 a minute and sounds suspiciously like his Aunt Marge. I'm sure there could be someone browsing through there right now who's looking for a girl just like you.

There are a few key words that you should beware of when composing an ad, like "queen-sized." That's a scary word. Years ago, the Queen of Tonga was riding in an open convertible with some little guy sitting beside her. She was a pretty big bruiser. I think they were paid by the pound. Someone asked Noel Coward who the little guy was. Noel said, "Her lunch."

I read that thirty years ago. I finally found a place to use it.

It's much more difficult for a young lady to find a man than the other way around. Some experts recommend hanging around the

but...

laundromats where all the bachelors do their wash. Be careful trying that. One of the girls from *Oh Really Orillia* met a nice young man there, and when she got home found her underwear was missing.

More dating advice.

Jim's guide to dating Fifties-style
May 19, 1996

It occurred to me the other day that writing these columns should be more than just a way to say something stupid and pass it off as prose. I have no doubt that after my demise they will be discussed at great length in English Lit. 101 at all the major universities as the zenith of twentieth century intellectualism.

However I realize that my musings do not appeal to some sectors of the population, like the sane, and of course, the teenagers in our society. I noticed that the other night at Oh Really Orillia, while I was trying to impress Danny Austin, a teenager, with my knowledge of women. He suddenly remembered he had left the bathtub running and disappeared.

Therefore I decided that I could win their appreciation by doing a column on teenage dating ... in particular, the first date.

Perhaps the single most important contribution I can make to the next millennium is to help the inexperienced teenage male to move into the world of inter-sexual relationships. It is probably better to learn from a man who has failed at every known technique, rather than read so-called dating guides written by Ann Landers, or listening to your mother.

Your first date will be the single most important move you will ever make in your life. One false step and every relationship you will ever attempt to form will be forever doomed to failure. One error, one infinitesimal faux pas, one momentary loss in concentration, will ensure that not only will you never have a second chance, but almost assuredly guarantees that you will never have sex in your whole life, without having to wait in line.

I only tell you this, so any young readers who are contemplating that first step on the road to a fulfilling love-life can relax and enjoy the experience.

It requires a certain amount of finesse to approach a young lady. Perhaps if I told you how I handled the situation back in the mid-Fifties, you can use it for a guide.

First, I hung around outside her house for a few days, careful to appear to be just walking by. One time she actually came out but I was able to hide behind a tree and she never noticed me. Once I spoke briefly to her mother. She was putting out the garbage around midnight. I stepped out from behind the tree and said, "Good evening."

After the ambulance took her away, I melted into the crowd and decided that perhaps I should wait a few days before continuing my quest. Finally I got up enough nerve to call her.

"Hello, Mary Jane? It's Jim."

"Who?"

"Jim."

"Jim who?"

"Jim Foster, I sit beside you in school."

"With the pimples?"

"Yeah."

"What do you want?"

"Do you want to got to the show on Saturday?"

"Sure, I'll meet you on the corner."

"I could come to your house."

"Better not, my mom just had a heart attack."

Normally that first date is somewhat stressful; mine was doubly so. I had made a slight tactical error when I picked the theatre. We went to the Opera House. There was a Dale Evans and Roy Rogers picture — lots of singing for the girls and gun-shootin' for the boys. However the second picture was a National Geographic film about some tribe in Africa who so far had not come in contact with the Maidenform Bra Company. Here we were, two fledgling lovers staring at a screen full of bare bosoms. I was caught as they say on a horny dilemma. Nowadays you can learn all about bosoms in Randy Richmond's column, but in the Fifties, this was rare stuff. I was too embarrassed to watch the screen. I looked at the ceiling, I looked at the floor, everywhere but at Mary Jane.

It's funny now that I look back, the subject was never even mentioned. We might have been watching Fred and Ginger. On the other hand what could I say? "I noticed Mary Jane, that you compare quite favourably with those African ladies"?

I phoned Tomkins and Branch and we went the next day. But we forgot it was Sunday and Orillia wouldn't have Sunday movies for another twenty years.

Orillia was the most puritanical town in North America in the Fifties. Ask your folks sometime. In the health classes at the high school they still taught that babies were found in cabbage patches until 1965.

I realize that this is hardly a complete guide, but O. Happy Day, the editor, won't give me any more room.

but...

Try it my way for a while and see how you make out — Oh, and don't forget to send flowers to her mother.

Love in the Fifties.

Sideroad love is key to society
April 7, 1998

One of the big problems when you were a kid in the Fifties was finding a car. There were only two or three guys in the whole school who had their own. We treated them like visiting royalty and were constantly bumming rides. Nowadays kids drive Buicks and Lincolns, but the best we were able to come up with was a '37 Dodge and of course, Dave Branch's '27 Chev.

Another minor inconvenience, we never had any money either. We were always pooling our wealth to try and scrape up a few bucks for gas. If you happened to be walking home from school and one of your friends pulled over, you could be reasonably sure that it wasn't your scintillating wit he was interested in. He was broke and his tank needed a transfusion.

Cars played a major role in your love life. Cars as a means of getting from one place to another certainly beat walking, but their true value was in being a handy place to be alone without worrying about little brothers or sisters.

My heart bleeds for the teenager of today. As the cities and towns grew, they wiped out miles and miles of scenic little country lanes that were ideal for mobile romancing. Developers have ruined romance for a whole generation of teenagers. No subdivider should ever be allowed to dig the a hole without first submitting a detailed map showing streets, sewers, parks, and liquor stores, but more important ... side roads.

In the Fifties, we were never more than five minutes away from a trysting place. Sometimes, of course, you drove for hours trying to find one that wasn't booked. On any given night, half the teenage population of Orillia was parked on the side of the road. The other half was driving around waiting for someone to leave. If the township had been smart, they would have installed meters.

Great care had to be taken in choosing a romantic hideaway. A friend of mine chose a construction site right across from the high school. What he didn't know was that the cops had been watching the place because somebody was stealing bricks.

His windows were just steaming up when a cop turned on his flashlight, looking for part of some guy's wall.

The odd time though, favourite spots got you into major trouble. Sometimes you drove by a buddy's car and he was smooching some other guy's girl. Most guys were pretty good if they happened upon this minor indiscretion. They might tell a few friends, but that's about as far as it would go ... assuming of course it wasn't their girlfriend that their buddy was romancing.

However, if your girlfriend was with you when you discovered this erotic little adventure, it was game over for Don Juan. Women have an unwritten code that a guy cheating on his steady dies.

Teenage girls do not adhere to the premise that a man is innocent until he is proven guilty. They prefer the Napoleonic Code that says, "an unfaithful boyfriend shall be executed and the details discussed at a hen party. If he is then found to be innocent, well, no harm done."

A friend of mine was caught one Sunday afternoon in the wintertime. Another friend drove by and the girl with him spilled the beans in the Star Cafe. He knew he had been spotted, but in trying to drive out, slid off into the ditch. It was amazing how fast the news spread. Within fifteen minutes, three or four cars were there, including one carrying his soon to be ex-girlfriend.

I think he finally married the girl in the ditch. Just as well really, their lives were ruined anyway. What with the big red "A" burned into their foreheads.

The Japanese have ruined the auto industry. Not because of their technology and workmanship, they just never understood the tremendous contribution Detroit made to romance.

First they made the cars smaller. Then the fins disappeared, and finally the old bench rear seat that we loved for so long was just a memory. They sacrificed comfort for styling and gas mileage. Now a love affair in the back of a Honda is borderline masochistic and no longer covered for back injuries under the Ontario Health Plan.

The back roads are gone ... and the quiet country lanes. The last of the great Canadian traditions has gone the way of the dodo. A hundred years from now, when historians try to piece together what destroyed Canadian Society, they will narrow it down to the tragic loss of teenage parking.

I thought people in Orillia were weird.

A view from this side of perfect
January 6, 1998

I'm sure that most of you know by now that people who live in California are a bubble off plumb. They are not exactly what we would call "normal" folks. There are hundreds of examples of their eccentricities, but one that comes to mind is a funeral I read about a few years ago. At the cemetery, the funeral director announced to all the mourners that the deceased would like to say his last goodbyes. He pushed a button, the casket raised up on end and the lid opened to show the late whoever standing there. I suspect that must have been the finest example of poor taste since Farley Mowat mooned the guests at Stevie Leacock's Awards Dinner.

I guess Farley has calmed down a bit now that he is approaching his dotage, but I'm pleased to say that Californians are still high on the lunatic list. This year one of their more popular Christmas presents was a gift certificate for plastic surgery.

Imagine opening a card on Christmas morning and reading,

Dear Cecil,

This year we decided to buy you something that you really need. This certificate entitles you to show up at the office of Dr. Sidney Glick on January 6, 1998, at 9.00 a.m. to have a few pounds removed from the big bugle that somehow ended up where your nose was supposed to be.

The Gang at the Office

Wouldn't that be a nice gift ... especially if you didn't know your honker was abnormal in the first place? After that, all you could do is go through with the surgery, or spend the rest of your life with a paper bag over your head — or if your nose really is that big, a refrigerator carton.

A few of us are very fortunate and have no flaws at all, but most people feel that they have the odd little deformity that they would have corrected if they could scrape up a few grand. The silly part is, the very flaw they might want to change may very well be the only thing we like about them.

If you are considering having a few alterations done, it would probably be a good idea to discuss the problem with a few close friends before you go under the knife. I'm sure that they will be able to find several other warts and defects that should be worked on while you are on the table.

Mother Nature has always been a bit of a practical joker. Sometimes she will hand you some great beauty mark. But while you are strutting around proudly displaying your dimple, your square jaw, or those baby blue eyes, the rest of us are secretly snickering at your ears, or that Adam's apple that looks like an ostrich swallowing a beach ball.

I used to love going to parties where I could sit at the bar and point out all the little flaws that my friends had. We used to laugh for hours about them. I guess no one has parties any more. I know I haven't been invited to one since 1964. I think it has something to do with the R.I.D.E. program.

Sometimes we are disappointed to learn that the "beautiful" people were not always born with fancy trimmings, but were helped along the way by a few deft strokes of a scalpel, or a pound or two of silicone. Dolly Parton and Pamela Anderson, I understand, were once reasonably normal in the chest area. However after a quick trip to their neighbourhood Goodyear dealer, they became the beauties they are today. They had to pay a penalty for altering nature, of course. The Air Safety Regulations are very specific that neither can fly above five hundred feet without being encased in a deep-sea diving suit. On the other hand, had either of them sailed aboard the *Titanic*, the old tub would still be ploughing the seas from London to New York.

Occasionally you hear of cosmetic surgery that through some miscalculation of the surgeon failed to come up to the expectations of the cuttee. A woman from California (where else?) was in to have some excess tummy removed. She later sued her doctor because he left her belly button off centre. I fail to see why this error was much of a problem. It seems to me that it could have been corrected fairly easily by shifting everything else over a couple of inches. I think she was just being picky. It certainly wouldn't be a problem for me. I haven't even seen mine for years.

Hopefully all these little abnormal body parts will be a thing of the past now that the medical and scientific community have perfected cloning and genetic engineering. Eventually we will all look the same. The only thing they have left to decide is who we will look like ... me, or Dolly Parton with her belly button off centre.

It's just US if you're from the U.S.
February 10, 1998

Sunday morning, the C.B.C was in Nagano covering the Olympics. The Canadian host asked one half of our figure skating pairs team how she felt a few minutes after she fell down during the short program. Only a Canadian would be dumb enough to ask such a stupid question. What kind of answer did he expect? The poor girl mumbled something about her disappointment and tried to crawl in a hole. What she probably wanted to say was "How do you think I felt, you jerk? I just fell down in front of thirty million people. This is the happiest moment of my life?" Our interviewers are right up there with Yogi Bear when it comes to bright ideas.

When it comes to televising the Olympics we can all take lessons from the Americans. No nation on earth can save a disaster like the Yanks.

Picture this: We have just finished the open downhill death run, where the skiers are sent careening down the side of a mountain with no ski poles and blindfolded. The winner was a Japanese lad, Sessue Hayakawa, who travelled the five-mile run in eighteen seconds before hitting the finish wall at ninety miles an hour. Second was Ole Olson from Sveden, followed by Helmut Schnecken, a young baker's apprentice from Baden Baden.

"Well Oak, (Americans always have strong masculine names, like Stone Phillips, Rip Torn, Rock Hudson, Pinky Lee — well maybe not that one.) Well Oak, that was quite a race."

"It certainly was Steel ... eighteen seconds for the Japanese boy, but I thought the class of the race was young Spencer Dweeb (Dem) from Fresno, California. Although he fell going out the starting gate and slid on his bum for five hundred yards until he hit the tree, he really had what it takes. Even when they took him away on a gurney, he showed the true Olympic spirit, except for the crying and shouting something about a communist plot.

"I like him too, Oak, But we can't forget the boy from Iowa who almost followed him. *Sports Illustrated* picked him for a gold medal. It's too bad he got caught up in the tow rope and went back down the other side missing the race altogether."

No matter who is in the race, on the ice, or hurtling straight down on a bobsled, Americans seem to be completely unaware that there are other countries in the event.

"Who do you see as the guy to beat in the men's figure skating final, Steel?"

"To be honest Oak, it's a toss-up. I kind of like Mark Wojohowitz (Rep) from Washington, although I can't rule out little Billy Barnsmell (Dem) from Savannah, Georgia. He's the American Dream, Oak. Would you believe that up until last Tuesday morning, the only ice he'd ever seen was in a mint julep?"

"I didn't know that, Steel, but here he is now. Let's watch. I see he's scheduled a quad and a flying camel lutz with a double-yoked toe hold in his program. That's a pretty big risk for the boy. Oh oh, he seems to be in a bit of trouble, Steel, he fell coming onto the ice ... looks like he forgot to tie up his laces.

Here are the marks ... 0 from the judge from Germany, another 0 from the clown from Canada. I think it's time we sent some troops up there, Steel ... a zero from the Polish judge ... wait a 5.9 from the American judge, that's better ... another 0, and another. I don't know Steel, there's just too much politics showing up at all these games. I think it's time we held our own Olympics and only let our own folks in."

"I see on the program that the Canadians have some guy named Elvis coming up. I wonder ... "

"It could be Steel, my wife was sure she saw him in a supermarket a couple of weeks ago. If he comes out with a guitar we'll go over for a better look."

Foster. That's spelled k-l-u-t-z.

Lugs and nuts just don't fit
February 17, 1998

Last week I made an tasteless remark about people who drive with their poodle dogs sitting on their laps. I've always thought it was silly the way Canadians pamper their pets. Today I wanted to watch an interview with Barbara Ann Scott on the television set upstairs, but couldn't. I was afraid I'd wake up the cat.

***

I have always been amazed at those poor souls who have no mechanical ability whatsoever. I'm talking here about the folks who are totally incapable of repairing even the simplest device, let alone overhauling a complicated piece of machinery ... like a car or a ballpoint pen. Whenever the Fates leave them staring at a smoking vacuum cleaner, a toilet that has decided to rise above its station and become a water fountain, or an electrical device that has suddenly become a cattle prod, they meekly phone a service person to come over at great expense and rescue them.

And then there are the other lunatics who know they have no mechanical skills of any kind, yet try to fix it anyway ... like me.

We had been noticing a peculiar trait of one of our front tires. For several weeks now, it was developing the peculiar habit of becoming flat on the bottom side. Apparently the top was okay. I figured that it was probably the quality of the air. I had been filling it with generic air from one of the discount gas stations instead of the good stuff that is supplied by the name-brand companies.

However, last Tuesday I was driving up Bayview Parkway and I noticed that the right fender was dragging on the ground. From what I read in the manual, that is a pretty good sign you are driving in the ditch, your wheels have been stolen, or you've got a flat tire.

I have never been all that fond of changing tires. For one thing, I have always believed if God had wanted me to do manual labour, he would have named me Buford and given me strong arms and hairy knuckles. For another, it's never been high on my list to see my name in the paper under the headline "Handsome young man found under car."

Of all the dumb things ever invented, a car jack has to be right up there with the pinwheel hat. If a jack really worked, it wouldn't be called just a "jack." It would have a good sturdy name like "Huge Hydraulic Lifting Apparatus" or "Big Bertha's Bulky Buick Booster," something that would give you the confidence you need when your car falls on you. All these devices work on the Law of the Lever, a shaky piece of legislation if there ever was one. It simply doesn't make sense to me that a little wee jack can lift up a car. Heaven knows what one of those things would weigh, but I would think almost as much as Marlon Brando.

The hardest part of changing a tire is not lying in the mud trying to figure out where to stick the jacky thing, or cranking it up without punching a hole in you or your floorboards. The hardest part is getting the stupid spare out of the trunk. First you have to find it. (Ours was hidden under the carpet in the back. I had never looked down there before. I thought that was where the engine was, or the piston-thingy or the spark bulbs.)

Then I had to get it out. That may be simple for a normal size person, but I have to stand on a footstool just to see into the bathroom mirror. Hauling out the tire got me as close to a hernia as I ever want to be.

Setting up the jack wasn't all that difficult. I had it up in just under nine hours, but getting the wheel off was a little more than I had bargained for. I pulled and pulled on the wheel, but I couldn't budge the darn thing. I kicked it, swore at it. I was just looking in the phone book under dynamite suppliers when Bill Skinner drove by. Bill knows all about mechanical things. He even has his own hammer.

Bill said that sometimes they get a little rusty and a whack with a hammer might do a world of good. He hit it once, took another look at it and said, "Sometimes it works better if you take all the nuts off it." I can still hear him giggling.

Life is tough when you are stupid.

Did I mention I was a klutz?

Anyone got a Phyllis's screwdriver?
May 28, 1996

I've been watching a major building project for the past few days. My neighbour Charlie Udell is doing something to his front porch. Every day they are out there ... never less than three guys, sometimes four. But so far I haven't been able to figure out what they are doing. Nothing seems to have changed. Except Molson's had to put on another shift.

I suspect the problem may be that Charlie is not the world's best foreman. His crew is always on a beer break. It's 8:30 Saturday morning and Don Wilkie just pulled up. Once Al Burgin shuffles across the road, their long day will start. I hope he's not late. The first beer break is at quarter to nine.

If Charlie had been the Master Builder of the Great Pyramid of Egypt three thousand years ago, they'd still be working on the basement.

I have always admired people who can build something. (I'm withholding judgement on Udell until I see if they actually finish whatever they are doing. Of course, since I don't know what they are doing, it's quite possible that I'll never know when they are done.)

I have no handyman skills whatsoever. I have been trying to fix a door on our garden shed now for six years. I stare at it for hours but it never seems to fix itself. I've been thinking seriously about sub-contracting the job out to Udell, but my wife says it has to be done by the turn of the century.

A couple of weeks ago, a major windstorm pulled trees right out of the ground and the shingles off a whole bunch of houses. For some reason, the door stayed on my shed. Yesterday afternoon it fell off when the sun shone on it.

Left-handed people are always crabbing because everything is designed backwards. I know how they feel because modern industries are no longer capable of completing anything and sell all their stuff "some assembly required." I don't know how to assemble anything. If I see that written in tiny wee letters at the bottom of the ad, I run the other way. For one thing I have no tools.

There was a computer desk on sale last year at K-Mart. But I couldn't buy it. It looked fine but then I found out it came in a box and I would have to put it together. Right off the bat, I knew that it would have screws in it with either the square holes or those "x" things. I think they are called Robinson's and Phyllis's but I'm not sure which is which. The day we took that in shop at the high school was the day that Jim Hill set his crotch on fire with an acetylene torch and I was too busy laughing and missed the lesson. (That actually happened. He survived of course, but to this day whenever someone lights a cigarette within fifty feet, he goes into cardiac arrest and won't come around until someone pours icewater down his pants.)

I have a screwdriver with a flat end on it but I had to use it to pry a nail out the deck. It turned out that the nail was supposed to be there and when I pried it out the railing fell off. The railing is still lying there because I need a hammer. I have two hammers but they are both left-handed.

Some of us are just not mechanically minded. One day last summer I cut my dad's grass. It's a heavy mower and pushing it around the lawn damn near killed me.

I got it out a week or so later and he was standing there. As I started to push, he mentioned that I had forgotten to pull the lever on the handle. That was the first time I realized it was self-propelled.

I think that there are a lot more of us out there than people realize. Every morning about fifty guys go over to Sonny Connor's gas station for coffee. I think that the only reason they go there is to watch Paul and Glen actually do something mechanical without cutting their fingers off.

We have one of those ceiling fan lights in our dining room. I'm afraid to turn it on. I can't remember how the fan works. I don't know whether a fan turning clockwise blows the air down or draws it up. If I turn it the wrong way, we'll have mashed potatoes all over the ceiling.

I can't get the light to work either. I tried to fix the rheostat but I think I read the box wrong. Every time I turn the knob, the furnace comes on.

Last weekend I put a new lock on the front door. It seemed pretty easy. But I put the bolt in upside down and when I closed the door, it wouldn't open. The back door was locked and Sharon won't give me a key. (We have only been married six years and she's not sure I'm a keeper.) I had to climb in through an open window.

Thank heavens, I still know how to run my word proces#@*^&%$/[{

This is probably as good a time as any to tell you the real story of Ireland's greatest hero

Pat sallies forth and tests his mettle
March 17, 1998

Today being St. Patrick's Day, it seems only fitting that we discuss the tragic tale of the Patron Saint of Ireland and why he went there in the first place.

Ireland was a peaceful little island when Pat arrived. Granted there was the occasional murder, but only of Englishmen and never more than a dozen or so a day. Most of the time, the peasants just sat around drinking poteen, a delicate brew made by fermenting potatoes and gunpowder until the resulting liquid ate a hole in the bottom of the pot. Once it had reached that point, a sheep or a Druid was thrown in. A week later the whole potful was strained through a sock and declared properly aged and ready for drinking.

There is a rumour floating around that Patricius drove the snakes out of Ireland and was promoted to Saint First Class for his efforts. Actually he drove the steaks out of Ireland, which is why they live on potatoes to this day. How he became St. Patrick is somewhat fuzzy. One theory is that they named a street after him, and gave the job to a French-Canadian sign-painter.

Not much is known about Pat, other than that he was born Patrick Cecil Bufforpington, was 5'11", 195 pounds, red hair, green eyes, size 11 shoes, wore boxer shorts, never married, had a nervous tic whenever women were around, spoke two languages, the first being profane, and was booted out of Grade 1 for peeking down the dress of the girl beside him. But except that, and his diary, little is known.

Pat was actually a knight and had come to Ireland to do a good deed and to test his mettle. Unfortunately, he didn't now what mettle was and never did know if he passed or failed.

Just outside of Belfast he came upon the finest establishment west of England, "O'Leary's Potato and Poteen."

The host, a genial old gent with a full set of teeth although not his own, poured him a forerunner of the present day Guinness, an alcoholic tar-like beverage that had to be scraped out of an oak barrel with a dory paddle.

"I say, chaps," said Sir Patrick. "Sure and would ye know (he had picked up an Irish accent watching old Barry Fitzgerald movies) where a knight could find a dragon to slay, or a maiden to rescue?"

The patrons looked at each other to see if anyone could think of something that would keep this Englishman there at least until his money ran out. They hadn't seen a dragon since they met Murphy's wife, and finding a maiden in Ireland was about as easy as finding a pork sandwich in Jerusalem. They hemmed and hawed, looked at the ceiling, then at the floor, until a voice from the corner said, "I know where there is a fair damsel being held prisoner by an evil baron."

Out of the darkness staggered a ragged muleteer who needed a bath almost as much as he needed a drink. To say he had seen better days was an understatement. His clothes were all torn and caked with mud and grime. From the lumps in his hair and the smell of his rags, it appeared that he had been sitting a tad too close to his mules.

"Good Sir Knight, but a few leagues hence, there is a maiden fair, who is being held captive by a cruel and most cunning knight. She is locked in a tower and cries out to be rescued. But alas, only the little people can hear."

"Who?"

"The little people ... the leprechauns ... fairies. You know what fairies are, Sir Knight?"

"Do I? I roomed with Sir Bruce. But where is this castle, thou scruffy and most foul-smelling varlet?"

"Pretty words won't get you anywhere, Sir Knight, perhaps though, a handful of gold would loosen my tongue. I see you have just drawn your broadsword and have neatly plucked the laces from my jerkin with it. On second thought, I must be off. Just follow the road kind sir, and would you be ever so kind as to keep the pointy end from my gentiles."

"I thank thee sir," said Patrick. "I shall sally forth at daybreak, but first I must perform my vigil."

"Oh great," mumbled the innkeeper's wife. "I thought I'd seen the last of that when my boy Michael got married."

Freshly vigiled and refreshed, Sir Patrick, after a delicious breakfast of potato pancakes, boiled potatoes, and a side order of spuds, mounted his charger and galloped off up the road to rescue the fair maiden.

Tune in next week for the great rescue and unfortunately the sad demise of Sir Patrick.

Legacy just went flat for Pat
March 24, 1998

Ah yes, we continue with the tragic tale of St. Sir Patrick. If you will recall, Patrick, freshly vigiled and rested, had just set out to rescue a maiden fair. (The suspense must be killing you.)

It wasn't long before he came upon the castle. It was your average fortress, about the same design as the Simcoe County Education Centre in Midhurst, but smaller. The towers were massive. The place looked not unlike Kingston Penitentiary.

He was just about to change his mind and go looking for an old lady to help across the street, when a voice rang out.

"Good Sir Knight. Sure and would you be looking for a fair maiden to rescue?"

Pat was a little taken aback. He had no idea what gave him away, unless it was the flowers.

"My name is Sir Patrick, Knight of the Round Table, Keeper of the Faith, Runner-up in the Camelot Open, Knight Errant, and General Joe-Boy of the Great King Arthur of England. I didn't catch your name."

"Faith, and I'm Seamus O'Neil and would ye be interested in rescuing a fair colleen from yon tower?"

"As a matter of fact, that's why I'm here, thou cruel and wicked villain. Release her or I shall be forced to redesign your vitals."

"Release her? That's what I've been trying to do. She's stuck in the tower and we can't get her out. Come Sir Knight and try your luck. The first man who can squeeze her through the doorway gets her, and half my kingdom to boot."

This was an interesting challenge. Even Arthur would be impressed if he could rescue an imprisoned maiden and end up with a plump beauty and half a kingdom to boot. Besides, Patrick had always preferred a damsel with a bit of meat on her bones. Whenever the boys were off chasing peasant girls, he could usually be found peeking through the kitchen window at the cook.

Patrick entered the castle and followed the baron up the winding stone staircase to the tower. He could hear the maiden singing from her lonely prison.

"Come to me my melancholy baby, cuddle up and don't be blue."

It was love at first note. He had yet to see this fair princess, yet he knew he loved her. He couldn't help himself. He burst into song.

"I'm wild again, beguiled again, a simpering, whimpering, child again. Bewitched, bothered, and bewildered, am I."

He ran up the staircase, his heart bursting with love. She was his lady. He could see the doorway — there was no door. It was leaning up against the wall. He could see her ... she was beauty ... she was ... she was huge, that's what she was.

The baron came panting up beside him, "Pardon me, good Sir Knight, I'm a little winded. What do you think?"

Patrick was trying to be tactful. "Well, she's not exactly anorexic, your maiden, but I'm sure she has a nice personality. Tell me Baron, why is she in there?"

"That used to be a pantry. She climbed in and started eating. We can't get her through the door. Get her out and she's yours."

"That's a pretty good offer, but methinks the Pope has the right idea. Right now, celibacy seems to be the way to go."

"Well, give me a hand anyway. There's five bob in it for you."

So Sir Patrick finally had his deed, the rescue of a fair maid locked in a tower. He squeezed in past her and put his back up against her back porch and his feet on the wall.

"Okay, I'll shove from here and you pull from your side. Heave."

Gad, she was a big girl. He pushed and strained until his eyes bugged out. The baron pulled on her arms, but nothing.

"I'll tell you what." wheezed Patrick. "Send in a couple of your men and we'll shove from in here. You keep pulling."

"Heave, heave."

Nothing.

"Baron, here's what we are going to do. Take some of that boiling oil you use for sieges and coat the door jamb. You get in here and I'll pull from your side."

He squeezed by the fair maiden and panted while they sloshed a few gallons of 10-W-30 around.

"Are you ready?"

"Okay in here."

"Now heave, heave, heave," ... PLOP.

"I'm through papa, I'm through, Sir Knight ... Sir Knight? ... Sir Knight? ... Papa, he's gone."

"No he isn't. You landed on him."

Thus ends the tragic tale of Sir Patrick of Ireland.

No one had the nerve to tell King Arthur of the tragic death of his brave and valiant knight. He just woke up one morning and there he was. Someone had slipped him under the door.

Don't you just hate it when great legends are destroyed?

Should Little John have been Wee Jock?
November 10, 1998

Another bit of shocking news hit the nation's press last week when it was disclosed in the National Post that — are you ready for this? — Robin Hood may not have been an Englishman, but a Scot. All England is reeling from this devastating piece of information and apparently the Queen hasn't slept in days. Well I'm sure she slept at night, but to the best of my knowledge, in the daytime, not a wink. This is one more blow to English pride that may be just too much for the plucky island nation to bear. First it was Prince Charles's ears, now this. It was bad enough when last year I had to break the news that Winston Churchill was actually Winstone de la Churchille, a Frenchman, and John Cabot was really Giovanni Caboto, a Venetian (the city not the planet). (Come to think of it, I never did tell you about that. That choice bit of gossip was in my Discovery of Canada column and it was so damn boring that even I fell asleep. I had to cut it.) But why did they have to go snooping around Robin's family tree anyway? Robin Hood is England's greatest hero.

This startling revelation calls far more into question than just Robin. Does this mean that the loveable giant, Little John, could have been, dare I say it, Wee Jock?

What about Maid Marion — certainly one of the great broads of the middle ages — could she have been Maid Morag? Somehow this Scottish thing doesn't fit. I can't see this highland Rabbie McHood swinging from the chandelier in a kilt. Well it just isn't done is it? I mean a gentleman doesn't hang from the rafters without any underdrawers on now does he? Although it's perfectly acceptable on the SHO Channel anytime after eleven o'clock. When Rob had Marion over to Sherwood for dinner, maybe they didn't dine on roast King's deer at all, they ate oatmeal and chased it down with Glenfiddich.

Robin has always been my hero. I have loved that legend since I was a kid. Sometimes when the missus is uptown, I borrow her green pantyhose and pretend that I am Errol Flynn doing battle with Basil Rathbone and chase the cat all over the kitchen. Anyone who studies the movies knows that Errol was the true Robin Hood and Olivia De Haviland was the only Maid Marion. This new kid, Kevin Costner was okay, but somehow he wasn't quite our Robin. Not only that, in his next movie, *Waterworld*, he had gills and webbed feet. Although they would have come in handy when Wee Jock knocked him off the log with a big stick.

Granted Kevin did add a bit to the original movie by swimming barenaked, which I'm sure boosted ticket sales to the ladies who sit ringside at the Chippendale concerts, and he did manage to drop some major smooches on the new Marion who was no slouch in the liplock department herself. All Errol and Olivia could work up was a peck on the cheek after Richard Coeur de Lion (Big Dick Lion's Court) gave his royal blessing to their marriage. Back in those day you couldn't get married or even fool around unless the king gave the nod. Richard was away for ten years, which explains why almost everyone in England had to wear glasses.

I read later that on their wedding night Robin fell out of their honeymoon tree hut and the marriage was never consummated. But far be it for me to start spreading ugly rumours.

I think his sexual problems had far more to do with those green tights he wore. I know that after I wear them for an hour or so, I get the uncontrollable desire to do needlepoint or whip up a nice soufflé, but that's just me.

But how do we know that he was a Scot? The *Post* says he was modelled after William Wallace, who would later become Mel Gibson. Can they prove that? He could have been from somewhere else. If he was Scottish and robbed the rich, he sure wouldn't be giving it away to the poor. He would have bought more Glenfiddich. Perhaps he was Irish, or even Jewish. The Earl of Locksley could have been the Earl of Lox. I know that's pretty corny, but if you sat all day in front of a computer wearing nothing but your wife's pantyhose, you would get a little strange too.

I hate it when some professor starts digging into the past and destroys my heroes. What if a hundred years from now, some nosy historian finds out that there never was a person named Brian Mulroney? As for Joe Clark, I don't think he even exists today.

I never would have voted for Joe. He has no chin. I would have voted for Hugh Segal, he has three or four of them.

I wonder what that is crawling across my ceiling.

Caught in the web of legends
January 13, 1998

I slipped and fell down our front steps last Thursday. I wasn't hurt but I decided to put on a neck brace and sue the owners anyway. It seemed like a good plan until the missus said, "Think about that for a minute."

But the crack on the head may have affected my mind. As I was lying there in the slush, I started to think of all the great legends of the past and what they mean to us today. If you take any of those tales and really think about them, you can always find some message that we can use today as a guide to our daily lives.

Take for example the legend of Robert, the Bruce, who liberated Scotland somewhere around 1300. He kept trying and trying to defeat the English but he always failed. The story tells us he was lying on his cot utterly discouraged and ready to give up, when he noticed a spider trying to swing from one beam to another. The spider kept trying but could never quite make it. Finally on the twelfth time, the spider reached the other beam and built a magnificent cobweb that is still hanging there today. Robert the Bruce got the message. He went out that very morning, fired his housekeeper, and from that day on, had Molly Maid come in every second Tuesday.

There are so many of these stories that should be an inspiration to us as we try to make our way through life. Who can forget the lesson we learned from Androcles, a simple Roman peasant who was walking through the hills and heard the cry of an animal in pain. He looked around and found a lion suffering with a huge thorn imbedded in its paw. Instead of running away, he felt great compassion for the poor beast and knelt down and pulled it out. The lion was eternally grateful for Androcles's selfless act of kindness and promptly ate him. From this we learn one of the really great Truths of life: mind your own business.

I'm not quite sure why teachers and the clergy are always digging up old anecdotes to show us how to live our lives. No matter what the story, they can always find an axiom in there somewhere that will help us face life's problems.

They can even find something worthwhile in Aesop's fables, stories that make sense only to someone undergoing psychiatric assessment. Probably the most famous of his tales is the Hare and the Tortoise. You remember the great race. The hare took off like a shot and was so far ahead that he decided to take a nap. But the tortoise kept on plodding along and the hare woke up just as the poor old tortoise was lumbering across the finish line. What Aesop left out was, the hare got a gold medal. The tortoise tested positive for steroids and was disqualified. Not only that, on his way home the judge's car backed over him. Now what kind of moral can a child get from a dumb story like that?

They can even find a moral in the works of Bill Shakespeare. One of the greatest classics of all time was Bill's knee-slapping comedy, *Hamlet*. Ham's uncle poured poison in his brother's ear. The widow, Ham's mother (Tammy, I think) in her grief promptly marries the uncle. Ham's girlfriend Ophelia drowns herself, her father dies, her brother dies, the uncle dies, Ham's mother dies, Hamlet dies. Everybody dies. Even Falstaff dies and he wasn't even in that play. There were more bodies lying around than a Bruce Willis movie. But what is really important is ... what can we learn from that classic? ... something my mother taught me when I was a little kid — never put anything in your ear larger than your elbow.

The strange thing about legends is that they are all based on something that happened or probably happened. (I guess the Hare and the Tortoise is a bit of a stretch of the imagination.) I'm sure that there really was someone like Robin Hood, or King Arthur, maybe even Hamlet. We know from the history books that Robert, the Bruce, was the King of Scotland.

What we don't know is whether nine hundred years from now there will be legends about us, and whether the children of tomorrow will be taught some great Truth from the stories of our modern heroes.

Preston Manning is in town today. I wonder if some day our descendants will read about Preston lying on his bed watching a spider swinging across the beams in Stornaway ... or Jean Charest, or perish the thought, Lucien Bouchard, as they wait to be crowned prime minister.

If it's Bouchard, I hope the spider gets him.

I try not to think about this.

Fifteen minutes of fame ... decades of shame
April 28, 1998

I think it was Andy Warhol who said that everyone would have their "fifteen minutes of fame." No one remembers the second half of his message, "and a thousand hours of shame and embarrassment."

If something embarrassing is going to happen to you, it is required by Murphy's Law that it happens when you are a kid. If it wasn't someone pulling your gym shorts down in a packed gymnasium, it was some dog falling madly in love with you while your next door neighbour was having the ladies from the church over for a garden party.

When I was a kid, Boy Scouts were a big deal. I know they are still around, but in the Fifties all the kids belonged because there was nothing else to do. We learned all sorts of handy things that I shall carry with me for the rest of my life. I don't know how often I've used my knowledge of semaphore ("flag signalling" for the uninformed), but offhand I would say never. By the time I figured out the message, the postman could be bringing the letter up the walk.

We took First Aid. First Aid in the Fifties was pretty basic. You must remember that medicine was fairly primitive back then. Leaches were still part of every doctor's tool kit and the main part of a nurse's job was to hold the patient down while the doctor was going at him with a saw. We learned to tie a tourniquet. Unfortunately we never learned to untie a tourniquet and by the time the scoutmaster got to the kid we were practising on, his arm had exploded.

My forte when I was a scout was knot-tying. If I had been on the dock for the maiden voyage of the *Titanic*, the disaster would never have happened. They'd still be trying to get the knots in the mooring ropes undone.

"How to start a campfire" was another bit of info that has served me well. Unfortunately I was sick the day we took "Starting a campfire with wet wood." Years later I tried to do it by squirting naphtha on a reluctant fire. Not only did the log light, but also my eyebrows and most of the hair on my arms.

Boy scouts were big on parades in the Forties and we were always marching to one place or another. It was just after the war and we had to be in shape in case the Russians landed an invasion force in

Toronto Harbour. What we were supposed to do when they attacked I'm not sure, maybe tie them all up with a sheep shank or something.

When I was eleven, Lord Rowland, a great scouting poobah, came to Toronto. The leaders were all excited — there must have been a free bar after. They held a huge rally in Greenwood Park. Every cub and boy scout in Toronto was there.

Rowland, the dough-head, realizing that he had thousands of little kids lined up in the hot sun, mercifully cut his speech short ... just over five hours.

This was before the days of the portable outhouse that we all know and enjoy today. (It always sounds to me like someone emptying a teakettle on a kettle drum.) Greenwood Park had two toilets. Some rocket scientist had worked it out that one urinal for every six thousand kids was a reasonable number. (He was the same genius who later designed Exhibition Stadium.) The line-ups for the can were only a foot shorter than the parade itself. If you had to go, you packed a lunch, and toting an empty milk bottle wasn't a bad idea either.

I knew I was just a pint off urgent, but for some dumb reason decided I could hold out until I got home. As I was squirming in my seat on the Mortimer Avenue bus, the dam washed out. I bailed out at the next stop looking for a bush.

Too late, I peed my pants right there on the sidewalk.

I can still feel it running through my kneesocks. It's amazing how hot that stuff gets. I think the engineers should be looking into harnessing it for the heating systems of the future. Of course, Ernie Eaves would have to figure some way to collect the sales tax every time you filled your tank.

As if it wasn't humiliating enough to squish the rest of the way home, there were people waiting to get on the bus. I'm trying to look the proper young gentleman with the Red River Flood bubbling out of my shoes.

If I am to be granted one wish before I'm taken away, it would be to some day stand with a full bladder beside Lord Rowland in a public washroom. He'd better be wearing his duck boots.

I had to write a column about our cat. She rules the house. In our household, I'm a distant third.

A cat is, well, no dog
August 27, 1996

The other morning, I was watching our cat stalking something on the kitchen floor. Duchess is a Himalayan, descended from the great sabre-toothed tigers that once roamed the mountains of Northern India. Century upon century have come and gone since that most vicious of predators terrorized early man, yet I could see that the same killer instinct was still in there, lurking silently beneath the surface waiting, waiting, for the moment when some hapless water buffalo or wildebeest shows up at our birdbath.

I watched, curious yet almost afraid. She had that same terrifying look in her eye that Health Minister Jim Wilson gets when he sees a way to beat some ninety-year-old woman out of her free birth control pills. I didn't want to see those razor-sharp claws tear apart her prey, yet I was fascinated by how quickly she reverted back to a savage killer.

What was she after ... perhaps a goat, a wart-hog, an elephant?

Suddenly she pounced. Ten thousand years of savagery concentrated in a split-second of raw fighting energy and courage. She was attacking a piece of fluff.

It was a horrible thing to watch. Just as she was landing, the fluff ... MOVED.

The cat panicked, her feet going nowhere at ninety miles an hour (like Wile E. Coyote when he sees a boulder falling on him), and finally catching a claw-hold in my bare foot, she turned right and took off behind the couch. She stayed there until the vacuum cleaner sucked up her enemy, then bravely sneaked out to look for something a little less dangerous ... like a piece of string, or maybe a sock.

Everybody else gets a pet that boasts noble ancestry, cats that fought alongside Napoleon, dogs that hunted with the mighty Sioux. We get one who's grandfather was the Cowardly Lion in the Wizard of Oz.

The grandchildren don't even believe we have a cat. As soon as the kids show up, she disappears. They think the only pet we have is two eyeballs under the bed. Come to think of it, when all the little monsters come to the house at the same time, it's probably the safest place to be.

Cats are too damn independent and cold. They are not fun things like dogs. Dogs are pals ... friendly creatures and sociable — like drunks when they run out of money.

Even if you have old Rover fixed, he still goes out girling with the boys. Although now he just goes along as a consultant.

Cats don't even make an attempt to be friendly. When you come home, you're lucky if your cat bothers to open one eye.

If you talk to a cat, it just stares at you for a moment, like you voted NDP, then goes on with whatever it was doing. Which is usually nothing.

A dog, on the other hand looks at you and nods his head as if you have all your faculties, which if you talk to dogs, you haven't.

People who try to carry on a meaningful conversation with animals worry me ... except for cowboys. Cowboys often had to talk to their horses to keep from going batty. Roy Rogers talked to Trigger all the time and then had him stuffed. I think he keeps him in the living room. Well maybe Roy isn't a very good example.

I talk to Rascal, Carli and Cuyler's dog. Not so much to carry on a conversation, but more as a rehearsal. If I have to make a speech somewhere, I try it out first on the dog. I have to speak to the Golden K in September, so I'll slip over tomorrow and run it by Rascal. If he laughs, then I know it's good enough for the boys in the Golden K.

Although he's not really all that swift. He's a clockwise Lhasa-poo. (Whatever that is.) If Rascal is on a leash and sees a post or a tree, he will walk around the post or tree clockwise until the leash runs out. Then he stands there looking puzzled. It would never occur to him to go back the other way.

Once he applied for a seeing-eye dog position that was advertised in the Packet, but he failed the test. Rascal got wrapped around a lamp post with a blind person, and they just stood there. If Mr. Gardner, the mailman, hadn't noticed them the next morning, they'd still be there.

Years ago, they started a seeing-eye cat program in the States, but it didn't work out all that well. It was fine until the cat saw a dog, then they had to call the fire department to get the cat and the blind guy down out of a tree.

Sometimes the cat would decide to lie down to have a little sleep somewhere and would leave the blind person standing in the kitty litter box.

This column is getting a little weird. Maybe I had better stop sniffing catnip.

My wife is ... well, different.

Finding the perfect candidate for a cat
June 9, 1998

We've had a blessed event at our house. Yes, another wee one has entered our lives.

I had forgotten what it was like to be a new parent, to be awakened out of a sound sleep by a little one's cry ... to lie awake worrying whether we can really afford another mouth to feed. So much expense. There's the cost of education ... and medical bills. What about religious training? I haven't been a regular attender lately, but now that we have a small one I may have to go back to see what the rules are. At one time we weren't allowed to play cards on Sunday. Now the minister isn't allowed to talk more than ten minutes so the congregation can get to the Rama Casino in time for the lunch-time buffet. But I have to learn all these things and pass them on.

Eventually I'll have to have that little talk about the birds and the bees. That's particularly difficult for me because I don't understand it myself. I could never figure out where the bird comes in. Come to think of it, I'm not sure what part the bee takes in the whole process either. Sex is dangerous enough without having something flying around that could sting you. And dating, what do I say to the little one about that? The responsibilities are endless. Another thing, what about our neighbours? Will he/she be accepted by them? (We don't know whether it's a boy or a girl yet. I can't see through the fur and Sharon doesn't know where to look.)

Oh, I'm sorry, you thought I was talking about a baby. It's worse, Sharon brought home another cat. Normal women go uptown and come home with bagels or silk underwear or something. Not her, she finds stray animals. If we lived in Labrador, our basement would be filled with orphaned seals and beached whales.

I have trouble with cats: I don't relate to them. Dogs are easy. If a dog likes you, it licks you. If it doesn't, it tears a big chunk out of your arm. You always know where you stand. (Although you may have to stand on the other side of a barbed wire fence.)

I don't understand cats. For one thing they ignore you unless they want something, then they rub up and down your leg. If a dog takes an interest in your leg, you know he isn't after anything, he's just practising. Call a dog and he will come right over to see what you want ... or bite you. But try calling a cat.

Dogs are trainable. Years ago the kids had a dog and they taught him to do all sorts of things: chase his tail, break wind, pee on the furniture, give himself a little bath in the living room just when the minister was there for his annual cup of tea. That was great — I could hardly wait for him to leave so I could crack open a beer and the dog got rid of him. One look at Happy performing his daily ritual and the reverend got all flustered, left his card, and hurried next door to try out their tea.

A cat would never help you out like that. A cat would completely ignore you or crawl up on the sky pilot's knee forcing him to stay for hours. Cats are sneaky. They use the litterbox for months at a time, then for no reason at all, hide one behind the couch. My wife always blames me. We could be sitting having a little chat about my shortcomings and suddenly she sniffs the air and says "Oh, and another thing."

Of course we aren't going to keep the cat. It's only here until Sharon finds it a good home. So far we've had thirty or forty couples over to discuss adoption, but there is always something wrong with them. Either they don't have a degree or there is something about them that suggests that they wouldn't be capable of raising a cat. The last couple went to Park Street Collegiate Institute, so they are automatically out. (That's not Sharon's idea, it's mine. I'm sure that a few people have graduated from Park and have gone on to lead a useful life, I just haven't met any.)

If we don't get someone suitable pretty soon, I'm afraid she will keep it. I have no say in the matter. We already have a cat and believe me, she's not all that pleased about having a stranger in the house and hasn't come out from under the bed since he/she got here.

If Sharon starts looking through name books I'll know it's too late. So far it's just Kitty, although somewhere around two o'clock in the morning when Kitty started to sing, I heard a few names from under the covers that suggested his/her days as a house guest are numbered.

There's another couple coming up the walk. We'll invite them in, but I'm not hopeful. The guy looks like a Liberal.

Every July, we get invaded.

Scots annual invasion arrives
July 14, 1998

This weekend our fair city will once again be invaded by hundreds of thousands of Scotspersons on their way to overthrow the hated English Government and declare their independence. Each summer on the third weekend in July, this band of revolutionaries pause in Mariposa for a few days to relive their victory at Bannockburn, drink heather ale, and listen to the mournful cry of the wild haggis. Normally Scots are a peaceful people, but once they hear an English accent or the bar runs dry, they lose all control, paint their faces blue and attack any fish and chip shop and English pub within a hundred miles. There is nothing quite as scary as seeing a wave of wild oatmeal savages, claymores glistening in the morning sun, running down your street looking for Anglicans to skewer.

If you have never seen one, a Scotsman is a horrible sight to behold. The women are all good-looking, but the men are usually ghastly. Archeologists and medical historians suspect that their long-standing practice of wearing plaid skirts without proper underwear and support may have destroyed their beauty genes. Their womenfolk, on the other hand, have managed to keep their traditional good looks by sticking to a spartan diet of porridge, oatcakes, and six shots of Johnny Walker Black Label twice a day.

However it is their music that distinguishes the Scots from normal people. Apparently some genetic disturbance passed down by centuries of in-breeding has rendered the population completely incapable of playing the usual musical instruments; they have only managed to learn to play the fiddle and the drum. They, of course, went overboard and formed massive fiddle orchestras consisting of thousands of mad violin-playing Scotspersons all crammed together on one stage. They can't even have a rehearsal without renting the Skydome ... or in Scotland, the Skyedome. (Only a Scottish person like myself will see the brilliant play on words there.)

That seems to be the extent of their musical ability, unless you want to talk about those other things, the bagpipes. Sometime around dawn this Saturday, a lone piper will greet the sun with an unearthly sound, not unlike the ancient rural Ontario practice of dropping a live pig in boiling water for God knows what reason. His lonely lament will soon be followed by a dozen more, until the downtown core will be filled with the skirl of the pipes and gulls and pigeons will drop like rain on Mississaga Street. This unearthly din will awaken the drummers who will rush out of the motels and brothels and pound away until the very bricks of our historic homes crumble like so much face powder, leaving the entire north end of the city desolate like Memphis after an Elvis convention. It also explains why every Monday morning after a Scottish Festival, every dog, cat, and squirrel in the city of Orillia is lined up in front of Ellis Hearing Aid Service for audiometric testing. But by then the Scots will have moved on to Fergus or Barrie for even more depravity. There they have Highland Games, where grown men run around in dresses and throw telephone poles all over the place. (Modern technology will eventually ruin the Games. As Bell Canada buries more and more cable it won't be long until there are no more poles and the highlight of Scottish Athletic Competitions will be two old men hurling touch-tone phones at each other.)

Unfortunately, the Scots speak a language almost unfathomable to normal human beings, which has kept them from taking their rightful place as world leaders. A few have managed to go on to achieve greatness. Sir John A. Macdonald, for instance, rose to the lofty position of Canada's first prime minister, in spite of the fact that not a soul in the entire country understood a word he said. His success started a tradition of incomprehensibility in our highest office so ingrained that today we have a prime minister who can't even understand himself. Just in case you should be in the awkward situation of actually having to listen to one of our gaelic visitors this weekend, I have undertaken to translate a few of their common expressions to enable you to at least carry on some semblance of conversation without having a nervous breakdown:

"Dinna ken" — I don't know. Not to be mistaken for the New Yorkese expression "Wads for dinna. I'm starvin."
"Breeks" — A type of pants that Scotsman wear in the winter time, made of wool and laced at the knee. If you should ever see one coming your way, hide your wallet, lie down and play dead. Finally, the motto of the Orillia Scottish Festival "Ceud Mille Failte" — An ancient gaelic expression meaning "Which way to the beer tent?"

Oh, yes. They come every year.

Wee Jimmy's guide to the fest
July 16, 1996

My friends, the time has come for Orillia to cast off the shackles of English Imperialism and become, once again, the Brigadoon of Central Ontario. This weekend countless thousands of pipers and drummers will come down from the heathered hills of Scarborough, Barrie, Midland, and all those other bastions of Scottish Nationalism, to fill the air with the blood-curdling skirl of the pipes and the beat of the drums.

It is time once more for me, wee Jimmy McFoster, to get out my moth-eaten old kilt, stand up on the hill in Couchiching Park, and gaze proudly out over the sea of tartans, wee bonnets, and sunburned faces, as we hold our annual war council to plot the overthrow of English tyranny.

This weekend, the City of Orillia will be Scottish to a man.

You have to understand the complicated ancestry of the average Orillian. Whenever some great national day is being celebrated, every jerk in town claims to have roots there and joins in the festivities as their designated ambassador representing the homeland — especially if there is a bar.

I am a true Orillian. For instance, last 4th of July, I was no longer Jim Foster. I was Jimmy-Bob Foster from Bugtussle, Tennessee. On the 12th of July, I became King Billy Foster and was arrested for leading a charge up West Street hill against Joannie Asselin and the Guardian Angels Church. On July 1st, Canada Day, I didn't know what to do, so I put on my French beret, jumped in a Japanese car, filled it with Arabian gas and drove to Buffalo for Chinese food, and came home with Mexican Montezuma's revenge.

I could go on. On March 17th, I was Seamus Foster from Donegal. On St. Jean Baptiste Day, I became Jean-Pierre Fostere and tried to burn down the Quebec Legislature. (That's how we patriots show our support for the our government: burn it down.)

But this weekend I will be Wee Jimmy McFoster from Glaski.

One of the highlights of the Scottish Festival is the Scottish Country Dancing. It behooves me to explain the complexities of this delightful pastime.

Scottish Country Dancing is like a sprightly precision drill and can be enjoyed by folks of all ages, from young nymphets like Cathy Kean to burned-out old codgers like Al Finlayson. (Of course it wasn't the dancing that burned out Al, it was being married to Margaret, a woman ever so many years younger.)

You will notice that all the ladies wear white dresses. This is because most Scottish women are virgins ... which could explain why the men wear what appears to be a furry jockstrap on the front of their kilt. It is actually an ice bucket — or in the case of the huskier chaps, an ice barrel.

It is required by law that all dances must start out in two lines. Any dance starting any other way is illegal and the participants are liable to imprisonment or being sat on by Sean Connery, or both. The male dancers (the ones in the plaid skirts) always stand on the side nearest to the bar. The ladies stand on the other in their white dresses of virginity, unless they are wearing a tartan sash which signifies that they are borderline nymphomaniacs and are only waiting around until the ice in the buckets melts.

The dance begins whenever a chord is struck or an Englishman bludgeoned to death, preferably the latter, and everyone rushes around until the music stops, or a male dancer goes into cardiac arrest.

Because most Scots are either Presbyterians or Catholic, the dancers are not allowed to smile or touch a member of the opposite sex. Any accidental bumping, especially of the hips, requires a written letter of apology to Rev. Eric Beggs, or in the case of a Catholic, a Lake Couchiching perch must be eaten every Friday.

It is not known whether the male dancers wear underwear under their kilt. Of course it really doesn't matter. Common sense tells us that any man who jumps around with 10 pounds of ice banging against his crotch is not going to be bothering anyone anyway. At the conclusion of the dance, the men bow to the lassies then immediately run to the bar.

If any amateur should care to join in, I cannot emphasize enough the danger of accidentally bumping or fondling any of the ladies. The men carry knives in their socks. I remember a conversation with Jock McLean, who was dismayed that Sikhs carry a ceremonial dagger in their belts (which I found odd, since at that moment he had a twenty-inch machete, a six-inch dirk, two paring knives, and a Black and Decker chainsaw stuffed down his kneesocks).

but...

I hope that this bit of information on Scottish Country Dancing, has helped you to understand why it is the latest dance craze to sweep North America. It is estimated that, of the possible 225 million people available to join in the fun and excitement of the organization, their membership numbers have now risen to nineteen.

I'm in trouble with the missus again.

It was just the closet doorknob
July 28, 1998

Women are strange. Oh, they are still delightful creatures and every man should own one, but you have to admit that they have very little patience, and even the little they have is short. A week or two ago (well, maybe a couple of months) my wife discovered that the doorknob on the closet was coming loose and needed tightening. Now to be honest I noticed it myself, but it was hardly an emergency situation. If you squeezed the knob and sort of pushed and lifted at the same time, you could still open the door. Technically, she did not actually *per se* ask me to fix the door, she said (and I quote) "The doorknob is coming loose." She did not say "GET OFF THE COUCH AND FIX THE DAMN DOOR." Had she done that, I'm sure I would have fixed it ... or at least gone over to Charlie Udell's to borrow a set of wrenches or a lathe or a hammer, whatever a person would need to tighten a doorknob, or maybe go to the library to get an instruction manual.

Today my wife informs me that she fixed it herself.

Quite frankly, I was offended. There are certain jobs around the house that are the responsibility of the man of the household. One of them is fixing doorknobs. That's about the only one I can think of at the moment, but the incident points out very clearly a serious flaw in a woman's character — impatience.

This isn't just something in our household, women have been snippy about things like that for milleimums ... mildendiums ... milllener ... mill ... women have been impatient for a long time.

I'm sure there were many afternoons when Adam was lying under a tree having a nap and Eve said, "The palm leaves have fallen off the roof of our lean-to again. I don't suppose, your Royal Highness, that you could get up off your big fat duff and throw a few more up there. The rainy season will be here in a few months. I don't want water running all over my dirt floor."

I'm sure that Mrs. Noah said more than once, "I don't suppose you could dung out the elephant's stall this morning instead of fooling around with the ham radio. I don't know who you think will answer anyway, the rest of the world is under 40 feet of water. By the way, the rabbits are at it again."

Granted, there are times when waiting too long turns out to be a disaster. Paris fell in love with Helen of Troy and their little affair started the Trojan War. The war lasted ten years. By the time the two of them finally got together, Helen looked like a bag of dirt and wandered around the house all day in a ratty old corduroy housecoat with curlers in her hair. The first thing she did was tell Paris that the doorknob on the closet was loose and before she would let him into her bed, it had to be fixed. He took one look at her, mumbled something about going across the road to see if Achilles had a set of wrenches he could borrow, and went to France and built his own city.

I'm not complaining, mind you. But women need to work on their patience skills. Maybe Georgian College could run a seminar on the subject. "Ladies, sign up now for 'If It Doesn't Get Done Today, the World Won't Come to an End.' — women only, $195.00. Please get your money in right away. If we don't have it by noon hour the world will end and it will be too late. Better still get over here right now and we'll invoice you — oh never mind it's already too late. We're all going to die and it isn't done."

What is that old adage? "If a thing is worth doing, it's worth lying on the couch for a couple of weeks thinking about it." Something like that.

There really was no need for Sharon to haul out a screwdriver and fix the doorknob today. I figure we had at least another week before it came off in our hands. Even if it did, it was only on the closet door for heaven's sake. So what if we couldn't get in there? There's nothing in there but towels and toilet paper. We could certainly drip dry for a few days until I got around to fixing it, and unless I'm mistaken, we are still on the mailing list for the Sears catalogue.

Doug Little, the downtown manager, got himself into a pile of trouble by gambling away 80 G's of someone else's money. I chose not to bring it up when the excrement hit the roulette wheel. He had enough bad publicity. Then the silly ass told all in Toronto Life.

Barrie ... I'll let you in on the poop
August 13, 1996

A couple of weeks ago, my brother-in-law, Jack, and I went to the big city of Barrie to see what life was like in the fast lane. (He's from Winnipeg, where the highlight of the social season is watching some guy slicing bacon at the Safeway store.)

As I was walking across a parking lot, a bird pooped on me.

People have often wondered why I have this great hate on for the city of Barrie. Well this is a fine example. That sort of thing would never happen here in Mariposa. For one thing, the smoke from the foundries killed off all the birds years ago, but even if one somehow flew by during a migration, Doug Little simply wouldn't allow it.

I was with Doug during a reading in Swanmore Hall, and of the hundred or so folks sitting there, not one was covered with bird droppings. Well, there was something on Gary Theiss's shirt but I think it was his dinner.

When I got hit on the parking lot, I asked Jack if he had any toilet paper. He said, "No, but the bird is probably miles away by now anyway." (I know that is a very old and very corny joke, but sometimes I get desperate.)

My wife is somewhat superstitious. She even believes that ad about curing a headache by putting a toad on your head. According to Sharon, me getting bombed with bird poop was actually a sign of good luck. Not only that, she had an itchy palm that day and that meant we were going to get a lot of money on the 6/49. When I checked out the ticket, we got zilch, the bird stuff ate a hole in my new shirt, and Dr. Pallopson had to put her on a prescription for poison ivy.

I'm always amazed by some of the stuff that people believe.

If you save the wishbone from a chicken and two people pull the ends, the one who gets the longest piece is supposed to get lucky — assuming of course, that it doesn't snap off and put his eye out. I suppose that's possible. Although if you think about it, it wasn't all that lucky for the chicken.

Blowing out all the candles on a birthday cake is also supposed to bring you your fondest wish. I did that once, and not only did I not get Cyd Charise, but I gave the mumps to all the kids at the party.

Another thing, you are supposed to blow out all the candles in one shot. That isn't particularly hard when you are three or four, but try doing it when you are a hundred. There's a rumour going around that that was what killed George Burns. He was leaning over the cake trying to get the back row and his tie caught on fire.

I always believed that you could promise anything, as long as you kept your fingers crossed behind your back. Then you didn't have to worry about it. Benny (the Butcher) Santucci believed that when he borrowed twenty bucks from Al Capone. When he wouldn't pay him back, Al had him made into a speed bump.

Some of the primitive tribes from Borneo still believe that having your picture taken is very unlucky since the camera can capture your soul. This of course is ridiculous. Although a friend of mine had his picture taken coming out of a motel with a Miss Trixie Malone. His wife got the house and the car. He was left with the kids and the mortgage payments. The last I heard, he had to take a part-time job in a circus to pay her alimony and if he reneges, the Ontario government will seize his geek's licence.

Some people believe that if you spill salt on the table you will have a run of bad luck. Your only hope is to throw salt over your left shoulder. I did that once in the Royal York and accidentally threw a handful on Mayor Eggleton. For the next ten years the only way I could get through Toronto was locked in the trunk of a car.

Breaking a mirror is also bad news. Even a crack in the corner means seven years bad luck. A friend of mine was in the honeymoon suite at the old Ford Hotel and the mirror fell off the ceiling. He got a concussion and a Miss Trixie Malone was turned into a jigsaw puzzle. Not only that, they had his Visa card, and by the time he got out of the hospital they had renovated his room, put new rugs in the hall, and run up a $300 tab at the liquor store.

So you see, some of this stuff is just superstitious nonsense, but some of it comes true. The hard part is trying to figure out what to believe and what is pure stupidity.

I read one time that if you wished upon a star your dreams would come true. So last night I went to Barrie and stood out on a parking lot to see if I could see a lucky star.

While I was standing there in the dark, an owl pooped on me.

A marriage made in Krypton
October 1, 1996

Well the world is reaching another milestone on October 9th. Superman is getting married. Apparently he and Lois are finally going to tie the knot after a relatively brief courtship of some fifty-eight years.

Maybe it was one of those Ozark wedding proposals. "You're gonna have a what?" At least they won't have to buy handi-wipes for the baby — they can use steel wool.

I hadn't realized that Clark had given her a ring in 1990. I must have missed the announcement in the *Packet*.

Mr. and Mrs. Waldo (Shady) Lane of Prices Corners are ecstatic to finally announce the engagement of their only daughter, Lois, to Clark Kent, son of the very late Mr. and Mrs. Jor- El of Krypton, foster son of the also late Mr. and Mrs. Selmo Kent of Sebright.

The wedding will take place at the Church of the Inter-planetary

Pilgrim and Bingo Hall on Wednesday, October 9th at 3:00 pm.

BYOB, no tank tops please.

To be honest, I haven't been keeping up with their romance, I sort of lost interest in superheroes when Peewee Herman got arrested in a surprise raid on a porno movie house. I must admit though, I have had some questions about the man from Krypton. I mean, what do you folks really think about a guy who wears blue tights and red boots? Don't you think that he'd be a whole lot happier with Captain Marvel?

Not only that, his mother made his suit out of the baby blanket he was wrapped in when he crash-landed and wiped out an entire year's crop of rutabagas. At least his blanket was blue: mine was pink. The folks were hoping for a girl.

I'm sure that there are some advantages to being married to a man of steel, one in particular I would think, but I'm sure that this relationship is going to run into a few interesting problems that some marriage counsellor will have to sort out.

We all saw the movie when he told the whole world that Lois wore pink drawers, but wouldn't you think that this x-ray vision could cause a little strain on the marriage? Everybody needs a little privacy now and then. But Lois won't even be able to slip down to the A&P on a hot summer day without Clark saying,

"My angel, I think you forgot something." Swhooooooooooosh.

"There that's better. I hope you like the black ones."

This super-speed will also be a bit of a strain on their wedding night. By the time Lois gets her shoes off, he'll be in the shower.

And take this super-hearing thing. It is a well-known fact that 99 percent of all married men have, on occasion, heard the missus mumbling away in the corner about some faux pas that he has supposedly committed, like leaving the toilet seat up or spending too much time staring at the girl next door in her bikini. But poor Lois won't even be able to think out loud without "I heard that."

On the other hand, it would be comforting to know that the guy you just married doesn't look a day older than the day you started dating in 1938. Lois, as a matter of fact, still looks pretty good and she has to be 80. She's the main reason that I bought shares in the Oil of Olay Company.

To be honest, I never really considered Lois and Clark a good match. She is, after all, mortal. It's okay for now, but Superman will probably live forever and I think one of these days her warranty is going to run out. I thought that he would have been better off with Wonder Woman.

I understand that the CBC is bringing that show back. Linda Carter has since gone into the eyeglass business, so they are planning to offer the part to Sheila Copps. Instead of spinning around and coming out in her Amazon suit, Sheila will make a promise she can't keep and spin around until she's re-elected.

I don't know if you realize that Superman was killed off in 1992, but was resurrected again a year later. I'm not sure how he did it, but I understand that John Charest is buying up all the 1993 issues to see if it will still work.

I hope the marriage works out. Some of the great star-crossed relationships do, like Bruce Willis and Demi Moore. They have managed to combine stardom and a normal family relationship. Except for the fact that she likes to appear barenaked on the cover of national magazines, they are just the same as the rest of us.

Although I haven't yet received an invitation to the wedding, I

but...

guess I had better send along a present. But what do you buy the man
of steel and his bride ?

Let's see, for him ... a can of WD40 for those mornings when the
old joints are seizing up, and for Lois .... what do you think about a
pair of lead pants?

Behind every Superman is a ...
January 14, 1997

We're stupid, you know. We should have seen this coming.

Do you remember a couple of months ago, I told you that Clark Kent and Lois Lane were getting married? Well if you hadn't got all juiced up over the holidays, you would have remembered. I knew this was going to happen. Here's a couple, dated fifty-eight years, got along just fine. Why did they have to get married?

So what do I see in the *Packet* on January 2nd? Superman is changing his costume. Now he's going to be wearing a white and blue outfit with lightning bolts all over it, and get this — "no cape."

How did this happen?

You know, guys. You've lived with a woman. Picture this: Clark is sitting at home watching "Jeopardy." A news flash comes on that a speeding train is out of control and heading into downtown Metropolis at ninety miles an hour (or in Canada, 144 km/h). Clark says, "What is a Colin McKim?" then zips into the bedroom faster than a speeding bullet and comes out in his Superman suit. He heads for the window ...

"Where are you going?

"I have to go Lois, I've got to stop a speeding train."

"Dressed like that?"

"What?"

"You are going out in that suit? Clark, how many times do I have to tell you? Red boots? No dear, not with dark blue, and that cape? Take off the cape, Clark"

"Can we talk later? There's a speeding train going to run over half the city, I've got to go."

"I laid out some new clothes on the bed, dear. I had a little chat with Giorgio Armani, and he's designed the cutest outfit. It's you, Clark. It's you."

"I don't care who it is, Lois, I have to go."

"It will only take a minute, dear, come on ... for me."

"The stuff on the bed? It looks ridiculous."

"That stuff is ridiculous? Look at what you are wearing. Can you imagine how I feel every time we go out to dinner and you are sitting there with red underpants over your tights? Clark, you are the Bill McGill of Metropolis."

"Lois, the train ... "

"So you say."

"What's that supposed to mean?"

"Today it's a train. Last night, it was a meteor, the night before, you had to beat up Gene Hackman. You're never home. I'm slaving over a hot microwave and where are you ... off saving people? I wish I could believe that, Clark, I really wish I could."

"I was, Lois. The story was in the *Daily Planet*. You ought to know, you wrote it. Besides, I was only gone twelve seconds."

"You can do a lot in twelve seconds. Last night you just reeked of alcohol. My mother was right, you're a drunk Clark, a drunk."

"Of course I reeked of alcohol, I took ten million gallons of light beer and dumped it in the ocean because the stuff isn't fit to drink. I never touch a drop of it."

"If you say so, Clark. By the way, you'd better tell that tramp Wonder Woman to change her perfume. It clings to your clothes. Oh, I don't know why I bother. This isn't working out, Clark. You're never home. Lord knows I've tried. I really have. I thought I could forget that fling you had with Xena ... and that affair you had with Madonna You threw your back out and were off for a week after that one, Clark. I was so embarrassed."

"Madonna? This is a comic strip Lois, I don't sleep with real people. Wait a minute, I don't sleep with anybody. I don't have the time. It's do this Clark, do that. Fly down to the store, Clark. Do the laundry, Clark. Don't forget to put the seat down, Clark. Clark, Clark, Clark."

"Are you finished?"

"Lois, I love you, but I can't go on any more. What am I supposed to do? Yesterday, I had to leave a cat up in a tree because you had dinner on the table. Last week, a jet crashed while I was under the sink, welding the trap with my eyeballs. I can't do my job. No wonder that other thing doesn't work. I don't know how to please you Lois."

"Well you could try on the Giorgio Armani, love. It's on the bed."

"Oh all right, anything to please you. This thing? Lois, where's my cape? My mother made that cape."

"Your mother dressed like a baglady. Try on the boots, dear."

"I'm not wearing them. They've got buckles."

"Put them on, Clark. You'll love them.

but...

"I look like Peter Pan on drugs, Lois."

"You look lovely, dear, now you fly along and stop that train."

"It's too late Lois, it just hit the side of the *Daily Planet*. They're all dead, Lois ... Perry, Jimmy Olson ... and guess what? We're out of work. How are we going to pay Armani for this stuff?"

It's about time you read the real story.

Bravo: The history of the strapless
February 4, 1997

WARNING: VIEWER DISCRETION ADVISED. THE FOLLOWING
COLUMN DISCUSSES AN ARTICLE OF WOMEN'S CLOTHING
THAT SOME READERS MAY FIND OFFENSIVE. THE WRITER
SUGGESTS THAT THEY WAIT OUTSIDE WHILE THEIR
CHILDREN READ THE ARTICLE.

A couple of weeks ago, I was down at the A&P and right in the
middle of the parking lot, I found a bra. I'm not an expert, but I
believe it was the Black and Decker Strapless Wondercup model,
with dual exhausts and ABS braking system.

I didn't use the full name for the "bra" here, which is of course
"brassiere," in the interest of brevity, and also the fact that I had to
look it up to find out how to spell it. I thought it had a "z" in it. Then
I realized I was probably thinking of "brazier," which is the type of
barbecue where most "bras" were burned during the feminist uprisings
of the Sixties.

Now I instinctively knew that this wasn't going to one of those
great discoveries that would electrify the archaeological community,
like finding Pharaohs tomb, or an honest politician, but I must
admit I thought at least the New VR might have been there.

Why was this bra lying in the middle of a parking lot? I suppose it
could have just fallen off. I have no way of knowing, but anything's
possible. I remember a rather embarrassing moment in my life when
the string on my pyjamas broke while I was standing on the porch
talking to the Jehovah's Witness ladies. That was twenty years ago;
they still haven't come back.

But I digress. After I found the bra, I wandered into the store to
see if any of the clerks were following some girl around. That's usually
a sure sign. However, the guys who work there are old geezers, long
past the age when they would be interested in that sort of thing.

None of the male customers were giggling and poking each other
in the ribs either, so I had to assume that she wasn't shopping.

It is a fascinating subject, when you stop to think about it. How
would this young lady explain a missing bra when she got home? (I'm

assuming it was a young lady, although I suppose a woman could wear that sort of thing well into her thirties.)

"Myrtle, where's your bra?"

"I don't know. I sneezed on the A&P parking lot, and when I looked down, it was gone. Why, do I look different?"

"You certainly do, the wrinkles are gone from your face."

Perhaps this would be as good a time as any to give you a brief history of the bra. I imagine that after the decision of the Ontario Court of Appeals last fall, we've likely seen the last of them. Twenty-five years from now they will be something on display at a museum, right beside the button shoes and leisure suits.

The bra was not designed by an engineer, although I read that Howard Hughes had a hand in it. An engineer would never design an article of clothing that opened at the back. That would be like building a Cadillac with no doors, and the only way to get in was to crawl in through the trunk.

It had to be the creation of one those lunatics from the fashion industry with a ponytail and a fan. The same guys who came up with the strapless evening gowns that befuddled us young chaps in the Fifties.

I should explain for the benefit of the simple-minded and hockey players that a strapless gown was a dress with the shoulders bare. The top was held up by sheer bravery, and in some extreme cases, adhesive tape.

Logic tells us that the standard "Over the Shoulder Jane Russell Full Figure Maidenform" just wasn't going to cut the ice. So as soon as they finished the atom bomb, the leading scientists of the Free World met at Jane's house to design the "Strapless".

Now mind you, in the Forties the "Strapless" was still in the experimental stage and a number of bugs had to be worked out. To begin with, some sort of support system had to be devised that could withstand the weight of the bosom without cracking one or two ribs. Since aluminum hadn't been invented, cast iron bars were driven through the top of the cups and anchored to the waistband by a series of girders and rivets. The resulting bra was quite serviceable. If it hadn't been for the fact that it weighed somewhere between forty and fifty pounds, it would have been quite popular.

However after several years of testing, redesigning, and some fairly major let-downs, they finally managed to come up with the

but...

lightweight models that today are on display in ladies' wear stores or parking lots at the A&P.

    Oh oh, my wife just said. "You dipstick. That's not a strapless."
Isn't that nice? Now I look like an idiot.

Omigod! There's another one.

Mental meltdown caused by brief bra encounter
August 11, 1998

Well, it happened again. A year or so ago, I found a bra on the parking lot of the A&P. If you remember, I picked it up and brought it home. I thought my wife would think that I had remembered one of those little anniversaries that women seem to cherish. You know what I mean, like the first time we ever shared a bottle of wine with two straws ... that kind of thing. I might have got away with it, but the tire tracks all over it gave it away.

Well, last Sunday morning I found the top of some lady's two piece bathing suit lying on the lot at the new A&P. Had this happened when it was called Miracle Mart, I would have naturally assumed that it was a sign ... a sign of what I have no idea. What I don't understand is why I keep finding these things. It never happens to Charlie Udell, or if it does, he doesn't go blabbing about it in the *Packet*. Perhaps it's a message that I should be crusading for the topless movement. (That is another big fooforah that went flat, so to speak.) Or worse, it might be a sign from above that I'd better lose a bit of weight. Apparently this can happen to a man as he approaches his dotage. What was once a slim masculine figure overnight rivals Dolly Parton in the chest category. I've noticed this with several of my friends, although not of myself. Where once, they used to congregate in the Speedo bathing suit section of Sears or Zellers, now they seem hang around the training bra counter in the lingerie department. Isn't it interesting that men stare at bosoms all their lives and just when they start to lose interest in them, they get their own.

But I digress.

This time I left the top lying there forlornly on the hot tarmac. I always felt bad about taking that other one home. I sometimes wake up in the middle of the night thinking of some poor lady wandering around the A&P lot with a flashlight searching in vain for her missing undies. But now I'm wondering if I should have picked this latest one up and taken it to the O.P.P. They might have a lost and found department out in the main building. If no one claims it in thirty days, it's mine.

A person can have so much fun with a thing like that. I could throw it on the back seat of my neighbour's car and keep watching out the window until his wife finds it. My neighbour is getting up there. I think he would be pleased to be even suspected of carrying on with someone.

I'm sure that a thing like that could have hundreds of uses, although a grapefruit carrier is all I can think of at the moment.

But enough of this levity. I think the city council should pass a bylaw that prohibits women from leaving their unmentionables on public parking lots where they are very likely to fall into the hands of young children or old geezers like myself. When I was 15, finding something like that would have caused irreparable damage to my mind. I might have grown up into some sort of pervert, instead of the kind, caring person I am today.

Some societies do not even allow women to wear such a garment, let alone throw them out car windows. I understand in some Arabic countries, ladies walk the streets with nothing but their eyeballs showing. That, my friends, does not solve the problem of males staring at young ladies on the street. What it does is simply transfer their lust to something else. A young man in say, Saudi Arabia, finding a pair of ladies' glasses on the street, would run right home and write a column about it. I don't even want to think of what psychological damage finding a woman's contact lens would do to a young man's mind.

I certainly don't want to get into the topless bathing issue again, but there is something to be said in favour of it and an equal number of opposing arguments. I know there a nude beaches in Europe and even a few here in Ontario, and they have caused no problems. On the other hand, some African societies where everyone goes topless also encourage their young women to put dinner plates in their lips. Can't you just imagine two young Zulu warriors leaning against a tree watching a girl walk by and one saying to the other, "Nice Wedgewoods."

Did someone mention booze?

Thish revooin' ain't ezee, ya'no
June 10, 1997

About a month ago I was in the Liquor Store. (Not for myself mind you, I was shopping for a friend.) Gord asked me if I had tried a delightful little English beer called Bishops Finger.

Gord is the manager and quite a nice chap. Although he can be very rude when you call his house at two o'clock in the morning. I think the LCBO should spend a little more time teaching customer relations.

Never one to resist the challenge of reviewing a new beer, I immediately scooped up a bottle. Unfortunately I hadn't noticed the price. Now I understand that they have to charge a little more for imported beer to help defray the costs of shipping, but apparently this bottle came over on its own boat.

I am not a good person to review beer or any other alcoholic beverage. I don't understand the terminology. We have all read restaurant reviews where the writer tries various dishes, wines and beers, but I never know what they are talking about. You've seen them ...

The wine, Chateau Grunge (1953), was obviously from the vineyards of M. Charlebois de la Maison et Fils. The bouquet suggests that the grapes (Vitis vinifera) had been hand-picked from the third vine from the fencepost on the north slope of the Rhone Valley and transported lovingly in a wicker basket made by the firm of Gaston Thibeau of Marseille, by Maurice LaPlante, the chief vintner, custodian, and village rubbydub. The wine had an unmistakable nose that leads me to believe that his wife, the lovely Collette LaPlante, nee Devillers, squished the grapes through her own slender toes. Either that or a dog fell into the vat. (LCBO. 26977 750 ml, $97.35)

So you can see that you can't just have any yo-yo review this stuff. It requires years of training and several replacement kidneys just to judge the quality of wine. You can imagine what kind of expertise you would need to evaluate beer. Which is of course, an infinitely more delicate beverage. But as part of my mandate as columnist, bon vivant, and fine dining consultant, the *Packet* insists that I attempt to raise the education level of this backward community until the average Orillian can hold his/her own, culturally, with members of the more refined societies of our country, like Hornepayne. Hence ...

Bishops Finger, +350702 500 ml. 5.4 % alcohol, $3.95 (I think it was $3.95. I bought it a month ago. Look it up, I can't do everything.) An interesting little brew, sort of beer-coloured but dark, about the colour of my brown pants, and tastes a lot like — beer. Yes that's it. There is a lingering and peculiar aftertaste that suggests that the bishop's finger might still be in there. Brewed and bottled since 1698 by Shepherd Neame, Faversham, Kent (Clark's brother) ME13 7AX.

I find that to properly evaluate any alcoholic beverage, it is necessary to compare it with comparable brands. For the taste test, I have selected a bottle of Labatt's Classic Wheat, 341 ml, Canadian, alcohol content unknown since I picked the label off. Representing another English brewer, a 500 ml can of Crest (10% alcohol) and rounding out our selection, twelve bottles of Dave's Massive Irish, 5.9 or 9.5% alcohol. I can't make it out, the bottles keep moving on me.

First I will clear my palate with a few ounces of Bell's Scotch. Now I'll take just a sip of the Classic Wheat. It's hard to get the exact flavour with just a sip. I think I'll perhaps I will knock back the whole bottle.

Tha's better. Moving on to the Crest. Randy at the Beer Store forsed me to buy this stuff. I thinck 10% alkah ... alko ... that dusnt look right ... alca — oh to hell with it. It's good beer. I'll jus drink little bit. Itz kina strong.

I can't fine the can, I set it down someplase. Oh here it iz, I was sitting on it.

Now we get into the Massive Irish. Itz goo beer two. I wunner who this guy Dave is? He looks like a grocer..makes goo beer.. oops I spilled the bottle on the couch. I'll jus mop it up. Can't fine a rag .. here kitty kitty.. a Himmalaying cat can sop up a lotta booze... can't fine the damm opner ..muz be here somewhere.... When Irsh eyes r smiling shure iz lie a mourn in spring..oh oh..i can hear a car in the lainway... itz the ole lady. I better shaep up

"Hello my love..I'm ritin a column. itz abou booze."

I hate to do this to another American hero.

Local writer helps Franklin
July 7, 1998

It seems only fitting just a few days after the American 4th of July holiday that I bring you one of the lesser-known stories of their great Revolutionary hero, statesman and inventor, Benjamin Franklin.

I just happened to be browsing through Mark Bisset's desk while he was at lunch and found a tape of an interview he did a number of years ago.

We take you now to Philadelphia, where *Packet* news editor Mark Bisset is about to interview a local man who has been running around like an idiot in a violent thunderstorm.

"Oh sir, can we have a word with you?"

"I suppose so, but I'm pretty busy right now."

"I can see that. I'm Mark Bisset from the *Packet*. You have been out here in this driving rainstorm for over an hour dragging what appears to be a kite. Are you having trouble getting it up?"

"What have you heard?"

"Nothing. I said, 'Are you having trouble getting your kite up?'"

"Oh that. Yeah, I can't get it off the ground. I'm bushed and not only that the buckles on my shoes have rusted and my plus-fours are full of water. Every time I get going, the water swishes back and forth until finally it flips me over on my back. On the last run, I went out of control, landed in some bushes and lost my dinky little pince-nez Brian Mulroney glasses. I'm as blind as a bat."

"Here, I'll drag your kite while you pump out your pants. Tell me Mr... . I'm sorry I didn't catch your name."

"Franklin, Benjamin Franklin. I'm a newspaper man."

"Well that explains it. Now tell me, Ben, why are you running around out here dragging a kite?"

"I think that there is electricity in those clouds and I hope to get it to run down the string."

"I see. And what are you going to do with it when you get it?"

"I don't know for sure but I've got the other end of the string tied around the handle of the wife's frying pan. I think I can hang it on the ceiling and read by it."

"You've been into the sauce again haven't you Ben?"

"Just a bit. But Mr. Bisset, I've noticed that every time we have a thunderstorm, the lightning sets fire to everybody's house. I'm hoping to invent something I call the lightning kite."

"I see, and just how do you think it will work, Mr. Franklin?"

"Whenever a person hears thunder, they simply have their missus run around on the lawn with a kite."

"And?"

"That's it. If my theory is correct the electricity should run down the string. For instance, at my house Mrs. Franklin will deflect the lightning away from the house."

"Won't that hurt?"

"I'm not sure. That why I'm sending the missus. But if I can't get the kite up in the air I'll never know if it works."

"I think I see the problem with your kite, Ben, you need more tail."

"Are you sure you haven't heard something?"

"Here I'll tie my belt to the end of it. Now start running."

"By George, you were right. It's off the ground and heading for that cloud. Look at that lightning."

"Do you feel anything?"

"Nothing. Here Mark, hold on to this string for a while. This frying pan is heavy."

"Nothing seems to be happening. Look, Ben, there's a big black one. I'll just fly the kite right into the middle of it."

WHAM.

"Mr. Bisset, it works. It works. Look at my frying pan. It's glowing. It's not very bright. Maybe I should try a pot. What do you think Mr. Bisset? Mr. Bisset?"

"I feel funny, Ben, and my shoes are on fire."

"Not only that, the lawn is smoking."

"In that case it's a good thing we are in Philadelphia and not back home in Orillia."

"Why is that, Mark?"

"You can go to jail for smoking grass in Orillia."

I'm a little worried about some of the crooks in our city.

Sometimes life's a witch
October 13, 1998

I was simply shocked the other day to read that people have been swiping sex and witchcraft books from the library. This is a very serious matter. Oh not the sex books, we can find them in a minute, just put the word out to all the mothers who have teenaged sons to look under the little lad's mattress. I'm sure they will all be there, plus a few other surprises as well.

What I am concerned about is the missing books about the occult. Four copies of the *Encyclopedia of Witches and Witchcraft* have disappeared. Now that scares me. There are a number of wackos in this town I wouldn't want behind me at the best of times, let alone after he or she has been slaving over a bubbling cauldron all day.

It appears quite obvious that whoever stole them has been casting spells all over the place. Someone has done a number on Mike Harris — he's gone completely off his ball bearings. Can you imagine anyone spending thousands on radio and TV ads about what caused the teachers' strike and actually thinking some dodo would be dumb enough to believe him? Not only that, I suspect that part of the potion dribbled into our mayor, Ken McCann's, drinking water at the same time. I can't quite nail it down to any one thing, but his handling of the E.D.C. thing makes me think he may be the reincarnation of Wilbur Cramp.

Instead of Inspector Jim from the O.P.P. climbing up telephone poles hooking up TV cameras, he should be sending his troops around to all the witchcraft supply stores to find out who has been buying all the newts and toads. (For the benefit of you folks who have not studied the occult, newts, toads, frogs, and some of the cheaper brands of American beer, are all used in the blacker arts, like necromancy, fortune telling, and conjuring up the fiscal policies of the federal Liberal Party.)

A good place to start would be the basements of all the people who bay at the moon and rant and rave against building a new curling club. I'm not a curler, but I can recognize bewitchery when I see it.

There have been a lot of prominent Canadians who relied on the occult to help them through life's day to day problems, Mackenzie

King for one. Mackenzie used to commune with spirits through his dog. Isn't that scary? The man who led our country through the Second World War was getting his advice from a creature who laundered himself in public. That probably explains why Winston Churchill and F.D.R. made Mackenzie sit in the corner on a newspaper at Malta.

I would hate to see this stuff get out of hand and we have to start holding witch trials here in Mariposa. I don't know if Judge Montgomery has had any experience in sorcery cases. Orillia isn't quite set up for it anyway. The only sure test is to throw the old dolly in a swimming pool and see if she floats. In some of the more progressive cities, they have Olympic-sized pools that could be used in the off-season for trials, but we would have to throw them in the lake and I'm not sure the environmental people would allow that.

Back in 1692, it was easy to find a witch. They all had a big nose (Karl Malden and Jimmy Durante wouldn't have lasted an hour). But now with rhinoplasty and other nose jobs available at every hospital or drop-in clinic, we have to suspect everybody.

I was going to suggest we hold another festival on Hallowe'en where we could burn a few at the stake. That's what they used to do in the 1600s. But we can't do that in Orillia. We can't even burn leaves without running into problems with the fire department, and we all know the stink Kelly Clune raised when the Rotary Club fired off firecrackers in the park. There goes one more money-maker down the tubes.

Now I don't want to get in trouble with the ladies again, but usually (how can I put this?) usually witches were women, and not particularly pretty. I'm sure there was the odd cute one, but as a rule you wouldn't find that many in a Miss America Pageant. With the men, it was different. Male witches are called warlocks and as a general rule are tall and very good-looking ... like myself and George Hamilton the Fourth. Of course, I could never be a warlock; I wouldn't be able to mix up potions in my cauldron. Not because I wouldn't want to. My wife won't let me in the kitchen.

So if you have one of those missing books, please bring it back right away. But if you really must keep it, will you please lay off Mike and Kenny?

Them's mighty big oranges and it wouldn't take too many to make a dozen.

Vegetables by the truckload
January 20, 1998

I read an intriguing article in last November's *Reader's Digest* about a man who was trying to grow a one-thousand-pound pumpkin. Which leads me to ask the question that is on everyone's lips "Does the world really need a pumpkin that weighs almost as much as Marlon Brando?"

At that time, the biggest pumpkin the farmers could come up with was 990 pounds. Then a lady from New York State weighed in at 1,061. (The pumpkin, not the lady. I have no idea what she weighs.) Now we have to aim for the 1,100 pound mark. I think it's a disgrace that we can put a man on the moon, yet can't even grow an 1,100 pound pumpkin. Think of all the things we could do with it................. I'm still thinking.

We could carve a jack o' lantern for next Hallowe'en that would scare the living daylights out of half the kids in Simcoe County. One peek at that thing grinning in your window and the poor little nippers would be in therapy for the next twenty years.

I should phone Doreen McDowell who sends recipes to the Senior Style, and ask her to whip me up a column with a few dishes you could make with this monster. In the meantime you might want to try one of mine.

Pumpkin Crunch

Preparation time — two weeks. Cooking time — nine days.

- Borrow Charlie Udell's twelve-foot ladder and with a fairly clean chainsaw cut a hole in top of pumpkin, being careful not to drop the stem on anyone. Lower two men with scoop shovels into opening to dig out pulp — approx. four days. (If City of Orillia employees, add two men, a supervisor, and two more days.) Save seeds for curling stones in case we finally get a rink.

- Shovel pulp into clean Champlain Ready-Mix Cement truck. Gently fold in a grain car of rolled oats, a case of butter or margarine (wrappers removed), two shovels of cinnamon, a one-hundred-pound bag of brown sugar, a pinch of salt. (If you are under doctor's care for high blood pressure, you may want to cut back on salt.)

- Blend until thoroughly mixed, I would think from here to Perkinsfield and back should do it. Pour Pumpkin Crunch into a series of clean dumpsters and bake at 350°F in the heat treat furnace at G.L.& V. foundry for nine days. Test by sticking straw broom in crunch. (I don't know why you are supposed to do that. All I know is whenever my mother is on a baking binge, she can go through a broom in four days.)

Let cool on back porch until December, then add a scoop of whip cream. Serves one.

Fat: the odd gram. Calories: quite a few.

Now I could understand all this lunacy if it was confined to pumpkins. Pumpkin farmers are known to be a little strange anyway. Well they are. Drive by any pumpkin farm in October and they have five hundred pumpkins piled on the front lawn with a big sign, "Pumpkins $2.00 or best offer." On the other hand, the lady from New York got $53,000 for First Prize. Some guy from Brockville grew the 990-pound one and shared $28,000 with his friend who grew a little wee one — 945 1/2 pounds. I'd be embarrassed to enter a little runt like that.

But in the article they listed all kinds of fruits and vegetables that people were raising to unbelievable sizes, a 900 pound squash. I hate squash. Every time Sharon cooks it, I smile and say "Oh my stars, squash." Then, when she's not looking, stick it down my socks, or in a plant, or feed it to the cat. The cat doesn't like it either. I don't know what she does with it.

Someone grew a sixty-four-pound celery. Celery is not the type of vegetable you eat. Celery is a garnish to stick in the top of a Bloody Mary. You'd need to mix your drink in a rain barrel just to hold a sixty-four-pound celery. Not only that, you'd blow 3.6 before you got past the leafy part.

There's a sixty-two-pound rutabaga. (I don't like them either. In fact, if it's good for you, I don't like it.) I'm sixty years old and still don't know the difference between a rutabaga and a turnip. There's a thirty-seven-pound radish, a thirty-five-pound broccoli, a twelve-pound onion, and a 262-pound watermelon. Can you imagine buying half that watermelon? Why, it would weigh (let's see 262 divided by 2, carry one) ... well it would weigh quite a bit. Some yo-yo grew a cabbage that weighed 124 pounds. I couldn't even make coleslaw out of that sucker without throwing my back out.

Why don't farmers spend their time growing something useful, like an 1,100-pound tomato. I like tomatoes.

A funny thing happened on my way to the scrap yard.

Sensible rules for highway drivers
February 3, 1998

Six-thirty a.m.

That's the most important hour of the day. Write that down. Six-thirty is the exact time in the morning that the lunatics hit Highway 48.

It was fairly peaceful driving last Tuesday. The heavens were still dark. The stars were twinkling away as if they knew what they were doing. Every now and then a shooting star or a scud missile would cut across the sky and I felt safe and secure because neither landed on me. It was the time of day when normal people were just waking and their little minds were filled with pleasant things, like how nice it must be for Monica Lewinsky now that she's famous, or how glad we are that our prime minister is a Liberal and has no sexual interests at all.

It was a wonderful morning. I was listening to Heather on EZ Rock News — big mergers, Mike's Milk had taken over the C.I.B.C., and the French's Stand conglomerate were meeting behind closed doors with the T.D. It was 6:36 and all was right with the world.

At 6:37, every bonehead in Ontario went by me at seventy miles an hour.

I'm not quite sure how it works, but I have to assume that every morning around 6:30, the members of the Highway 48 Kamikaze Club slip out of the local mental institutions and quietly form up in big long lines along the sideroads ... lights out of course, so as to not wake up the guards. They sit there waiting, occasionally revving their pick-ups, or adding one more rubber hula doll to the dozen or so already hanging on their rearview mirror. Maybe they take another hit from last night's bottle of Old Porchclimber, or check their tooth, but they lurk there in the darkness impatiently watching or listening for the signal. I don't know what the signal is ... a flare perhaps, the flash of a starting pistol, or a command from Jack Latimer, but something happens at precisely 6:37. Suddenly it's the Molson's 500 and every inch of pavement from Beaverton to Sutton is teeming with panic-stricken maniacs trying to make it to the pencil factory in Mississauga by seven o'clock.

Highway drivers fascinate me, but did I miss a change in the Traffic Act? I thought there some requirement that you had to be able to read? The metric system still baffles me, but I'm fairly sure a sign saying sixty kilometres per hour doesn't mean eighty miles per hour. "Passing lane" doesn't mean a 1973 Ford Pick-up and a tractor trailer can go by you at the same time.

Wasn't there a rule that anything barrelling down the highway in the middle of the night had to have lights, or was that just a recommendation? I thought a flashing red light mean stop, not close your eyes and take a run at it.

As Matt Dillon used to say, "Times they are a-changing."

Maybe it's because I'm an old geezer and get befuddled, but do you really think the guy who came up with the passing strip down the middle of a four-lane highway had all his marbles? I'm talking about the genius who designed suicide alley along Barrie's Bayfield Street. Did it not occur to the Planning Division of the Department of Highways, that painting arrows on the pavement is confusing at the best of times, but in the winter it's sheer lunacy? Does the word "snow" ring a bell down there? I suspect that the Government may have gone a little overboard when they hired all the immigrants.

"Now, Mr. Valdez, I see you have designed a road before. Just where was that?"

"Columbia, señor."

"Wonderful. We can use a man with your experience. Have you ever heard of Cochrane, Mr. Valdez ?"

I have a few rule changes to help make it just a little safer to be on the highways.

1) Anyone driving with a signal light still on after passing through an intersection will be shot.
2) Anyone who passes someone on the highway, then slows down to a crawl, will be shot.
3) Anyone driving at, or under, the speed limit in the passing lane will be shot.
4) Anyone pulling onto a major highway without looking, will be shot, or run over and then shot.
5) Anyone driving on a major highway with a poodle on their lap will be shot. The dog will be clipped, shampooed, and then shot.

but...

Finally,

5) If I ever drive near Sutton at 6:37 in the morning again, I'll send my little black book of phone numbers to Bill Clinton and I'll shoot myself.

Overlooked again.

Slow pitching for a nomination
January 16, 1996

Once again the nominations for the Athlete of the Year have come and gone, and once again I wasn't nominated.

It's sad really, that a person like myself would be overlooked all these years for the simple reason that I have no athletic skills whatsoever.

Now I have nothing against the people nominated. As a matter of fact I rather admire them for their hours of dedication and practice, their grueling training programs, their constant striving for perfection.

But evidently no thought has been given to presenting an award every year to the athlete, who in spite of trying every major sport except nude mud-wrestling, has mastered none of them.

Not that I didn't try. I might have made it to the NHL but for a minor problem with skating — I couldn't.

Well, it was different when I was a kid back in Toronto. We had nowhere to play. I suppose you could always go to one of the outdoor rinks but it was cold out there and it was hard to impress the girls when your nose was running all the time.

When we moved to Orillia, I skated a couple of times, but the little kids kept knocking me down.

So I tried basketball for a few years but even then I had problems. For one thing I was so short I couldn't slam dunk a wastepaper basket, and for another, the little kids kept knocking me down.

Oh it was fine for Doolittle and Tomkins and Deverell, they were bigger, but when the little kids had finished with me, then they knocked me down.

Jim Nichol was the same size as I was. The only guy we liked to play with was Bill Doherty. He was really small. But Billy went away for a while and when he came back he was about 5'11". I hid in the basement for a year and Jim moved to Coldwater.

Football was probably what I would call my universal sport — everybody knocked me down.

I've been wondering if the city might consider a category in the Athlete of the Year Awards for somebody who was no good at anything, but knows someone who is ... or was.

What if next year I was nominated for Athlete of the Year because my brother-in-law ran in the Olympics. That was back in '56 when the Olympics were the real Olympics. The Games were a lot purer then than they are now. That was before all the scandals.

In '56, steroids were something you played your Guy Lombardo records on. Hemorrhoids were what you got from sitting around all day listening to Guy Lombardo on your steroids.

I always thought that a real good job would be a urine donor for Ben Johnson. No matter what you had, it had to run clearer than Ben.

In '56 all Olympic athletes were amateurs. They still are, but the definition of amateur has been modified slightly. Back then an amateur was a person who had never received money for playing in an athletic event. The rules now suggest that an amateur is any athlete who received less than a quarter of a million in endorsements in any given year.

Of course there weren't as many events in '56. Let's see, there was run in a circle, run in a straight line, jump over a stick, throw a spear at another guy ... and oh yeah, Greco-Roman wrestling. That was two guys wrestling barenaked — you've all seen the statues. It was finally banned and as far as I know is only found in San Francisco and at a couple of bars in downtown Toronto.

Now sadly, the Olympics just aren't the same anymore. They've let in so many wimpy events — the three-legged race, flower arrangement. A guy with an earring got a gold medal in Atlanta for knitting his own underwear.

I like to watch the synchronized swimming, but tell me, if one of them drowns, do they all have to?

I saw a commercial the other day where the whole team was showering together ... all synchronized. That's carrying togetherness too far. If one of them gets married, the groom better eat a lot of eggs.

Maybe I'm just one of those guys who can't let go of the past. I was reminiscing with Stan Craig one day. Stan was one of the guys who played ball in the Industrial League in the park before every wimp got to wear a glove. The subject got around to slowpitch and I said that it is a wonderful game. It gives a grandfather and his granddaughter the opportunity to play on the same team.

So whoever wins the award this year, congratulations. But don't expect to win it next year. I'm a cinch — unless some big kids knock me down.

Why is the pavement on fire?

Planning for a heat wave
May 12, 1998

I was sitting on my porcelain reading chair browsing through an old copy of _Reader's Digest_ when an item caught my eye that filled me with the same sense of panic as that letter from Revenue Canada. It was in an article called "Answers to Everyday Mysteries." It said that five billion years from now, the sun will convert all its hydrogen fuel into helium and change to a red giant. Its diameter will extend far beyond the orbit of the earth and burn us all to a cinder.

Now isn't that a nice thing to read first thing in the morning? Here we are spending all this time and money planting flowers and now the sun is going to fry us like so much bacon ... and probably do serious damage to our petunias to boot. Why didn't someone tell us this was going to happen before we bought all those seeds? Surely it was the responsibility of the flower person to warn us of this impending disaster. Right there on the side of the packet of chrysanthermoniums, it says "avoid direct sunlight or temperatures in excess of 27,000,000°F." (That's in wee small print like the line in my 1962 Ford Anglia book that said "should this vehicle be driven over twenty-five miles per hour, all warranties shall be null and void.")

Another thing: if the sun turns to helium, will all our voices go squeaky? I can't imagine living in a world where everybody sounds like Preston Manning.

Sharon has been bugging me to cut the lawn. I had pencilled it in for sometime late July, but it hardly seems worth it now. I was also going to paint the house someday. There's no sense doing that if it is only going to be burnt to a crisp. I was supposed to stain the deck, but not now. By the time I finally get around to doing it, the world will look like the bagel I tried to warm up under the broiler just as "Baywatch" was coming on. It was black ... and very wet. Bob Fletcher was in charge of the fire call and he turned the hose right through our kitchen window. (They retired him after that and if my wife gets a hold of him, they'll be retreading him too.)

I know it sounds like a long time, five billion years, but you know how the hours slip by. It seems like only yesterday that I was sitting in the backyard sipping on a bottle of Canvasback Ale and now it's gone and I don't get my allowance until Friday. As a matter of fact, it was yesterday.

Does Walmart know about this? They sure aren't going to build a new store if the damn thing is going to catch fire in five billion years. I hope the guy who bought the old Woolworth store doesn't hear about it. Although he might be okay; I understand it has a sprinkler system.

What's going to happen to our new curling club? Now the council has one more reason to put off making a decision. I long ago lost track of who the good guys are and who is holding it up, but I guess it won't matter anymore. It's hard enough to keep ice in the wintertime, imagine what a 27,000,000°F heat wave will do to it. I don't know much about curling (I was into the more manly sports like needlepoint), but I'm sure that it will be hell on wheels trying to sweep sweep sweep when your broom is on fire.

On the other hand, there is a good side to all this. The city's snowplow budget will be almost nil. The debate over whether or not to spray the park with insecticide will finally be over since the grass will be burned to a crisp. And at last we'll get an incinerator that the C.A.E (Citizens Against Everything) won't protest. Unfortunately we'll all be in it.

The annual Victoria Day sidewalk sale will no longer be in danger of being rained out. I can almost guarantee the merchants won't be standing out on Mississaga Street, looking up at the clouds, wondering whether to haul in the racks of last summer's merchandise to be stored away until the Leacock Days annual sidewalk sale in August. Instead they will be standing there wondering why their umbrella is on fire.

On the other hand, I suppose we better start preparing for the big fireball. It wouldn't be a bad idea to call your insurance agent and ask whether your homeowner's policy has any small print to cover a sudden temperature rise of 27,000,000 degrees. I called Maurice McParland just to make sure my life insurance will still be in effect. He assured me that it would. They will just issue an asbestos cheque. Of course the bank machine will be melted and I won't be able to cash it. Come to think of it, I'll be toast anyway, it will be Sharon's problem.

In the meantime, I'll head over to Charlie Udell's and break the news to him. He was crabbing the other day about it being too cool to sit out in the evening. Wait till he hears about the 27,000,000-degree firestorm coming this way. That will shut him up.

A horse of a different colour is ... well pretty ridiculous if it's blue.

A column that is so cliché
May 19, 1998

Have you ever wondered where all the clichés came from? Neither have I. I'm sure though by using a little common sense, I can take the bull by the horns, fight the good fight, and with no beating around the bush, figure them out. And just in the nick of time too, you wouldn't want to kick the bucket not knowing why we should never "look a gift horse in the mouth." What does this ridiculous expression mean anyway, and where did it come from?

It's quite simple really. Once in a blue moon, we receive gifts for almost no reason. That very thing happened many centuries ago, just outside the city of Troy. If you recall, the Greeks under Agamemnon, Achilles, or Jimmy the Greek, held Troy under siege for ten years. The Greeks built a huge wooden horse and left it outside the city gates. The Trojans, being a little shy on grey matter, hauled it inside. While they were peeking in the mouth trying to find out where the giggling was coming from, the Greeks climbed out the rear end and put them to the sword. From this we learn a valuable lesson, "Never look a gift horse in the mouth." I thought of a better one but this is a family newspaper.

People often ask me, "Mr. Foster, what does it mean 'to save one's bacon'?" Years ago, before we had a stable economy based on the loonie, a coin useful now only for parking metres and bubble gum machines, a person's retirement was based on food. Financial advisors sold RBSPs (Registered Bacon Savings Plans). Every February, people lined up outside banks, trust companies, credit unions, and cold storage lockers, with cartloads of food to salt away for their retirement. Otherwise Revenue Canada would come into their hovels in April and clean out the fridge. Since bacon was smoked it was likely to last a few days longer than say, a slice of Spam, or a hunk of Polish sausage, and so most folks saved it for their old age ... which was at that time, around 20. Hence, we say, "to save one's bacon."

"Eat crow" was a similar expression and referred to those persons who gobbled up everything in sight while they were young, relying on the government to feed them when they retired. In those days, governments helped the poor. This was common until The Harris came out of the north and cooked their goose. Without a warehouse full of bacon, pensioners had zilch to eat and survived by shooting blackbirds. The really desperate were forced to eat Brussels sprouts, the lowest rung on the food chain, just under grubs and dung beetles.

As you can see, most clichés are based on everyday activities or events. Some however are not quite as logical as these first few and may even sound stupid.

A classic example, "put your money where your mouth is," although a somewhat self-explanatory expression, has been passed down to us from the early Britons. Centuries ago, the average English peasant had no place to keep his coins while out walking. Since no one had any money in the first place, it really wasn't that much of a problem until the industrial revolution. Then rich factory owners began the practice of paying vast sums of money to workers to slug away at their looms from dawn till dusk. Suddenly it became necessary for the average man to find some place to hold his money. (This was never a problem in Orillia since our robber barons never paid anyone enough money to worry about.)

In the dark ages, purses were commonplace and it was considered fairly respectable for a man to be seen with a shoulder bag, although carrying a beaded handbag was looked on with a jaundiced eye and his membership in the YMCA would likely be cancelled. Later the whole practice was frowned upon and purses disappeared from the mainstream of acceptable menswear until the 1980s, when a guy with a ponytail on Fashion TV came up with one to match his lavender pixie boots. They are now considered *haute couture* in almost every community where men and women wear matching outfits and earrings.

Surprisingly, the first article designed solely to hold money was the common wallet used in France in 1763. However it proved totally impractical until 1833 when Napoleon Bonaparte invented the pocket. As you might expect, the wallet was hardly off the drawing board when someone dreamed up pickpocketry, a profession on the social scale just above Government Finance Minister.

Rather than risk having someone's dirty digits rooting around his pocket fishing for loose change, it became quite common for a traveller to keep excess coins in his mouth. Inevitably accidents would happen and more than a few wayfarers in a moment of fright or confusion swallowed their loonies. Which of course now gave us two clichés: "put your money where your mouth is" and "pass the buck."

A thing of beauty is a joy forever ... although Zsa Zsa could do with another facelift.

What is acceptable in today's world?
June 2, 1998

I have a great deal of difficulty describing women. It's a flaw I must have been born with — I have never been able to do it. I've been working on a series of books that I hope someday my agent can pawn off on a publisher. He likes the way I describe women. Of course he is one of those guys you see hanging around the girlie section of the United Cigar Store with a razor blade and a magnifying glass.

But what is acceptable in a family newspaper? I can always ask Ken Koyama the publisher, but he came here from Orangeville. What do hicks from Orangeville know about women ... or anything else for that matter? You're not a hick, Ken. I meant all the rest of them. Really ... I'm sorry I brought it up.

There is a character in one of my stories, Eleanor Bugwhistle. She is without a doubt the most beautiful girl in all of eleventh-century England. I know it. All the men in the book know it. But I can't seem to be able to describe her so that you the reader (or in the case of anyone educated at West Ward School, the listener) knows it.

"He was overwhelmed by her beauty. The girl was exquisite, the very essence of all that is pure and lovely. Her eyes, the endless blue of a winter sky ... her silken hair cascaded down over her graceful shoulders like a radiant river of white gold. Each shining strand caught the rays of the sun-filled sky behind her, forming an iridescent halo around her perfect face ... blah, blah, blah."

Now be honest, have you ever heard anything so sappy in all your life? All my female characters have to be blondes because I can't think of any way to describe brunettes. If they don't have golden hair, they're out of luck. Girls with brown hair are even worse. I can get by with "raven-black tresses" but what can I say about some poor lass whose been stuck with locks the colour of hiking boots? I like brown hair so don't start phoning the *Packet*, I just don't know how to write about it.

"Her BROWN stringy hair cascaded down over her shoulders like a radiant river of Hortons coffee left for days in a paper cup. Her BROWN hair sat on her head like ... like ... like bean sprouts left in the box too long." For some reason it doesn't sound all that sexy.

What kind of reader would get turned on by stuff like that? And when was the last time you told the missus that an iridescent halo framed her perfect face. You would be more likely to say "Those pimples are back again. I told you to lay off the chocolate eclairs."

How do you describe a woman's nose? It's easy to talk about a man's. "He was an average sort of chap, with a honker the size of cantaloupe right in the middle of his handsome puss."

Some writers are so perverted that they even describe women's ears. My female characters always have long hair, then I don't have to worry about it. Imagine some bozo talking about the beauty of some lady's ears. Unless you are some sort of freak, or an ears, nose, and throat specialist, who even looks at them?

What is acceptable nowadays when describing the female form ... especially in a community like ours? I don't want the Business Women's Association or a phalanx from the I.O.D.E. parading along Colborne Street demanding my head.

Are we allowed to mention bottoms these days? I don't know. And what about bosoms?

I once wrote "In came a fiddler, followed by Mrs. Fezziwig, a big mama with huge ... picture two zeppelins landing side by side at Pearson Airport." Is that acceptable in the *Packet*?

In the big city papers they are allowed to write about Viagra and the effect it has on those things that men have. I wouldn't dare say that word in Orillia, or what the Viagra does to them either. That's not a problem here anyway. In Orillia, men don't even think about that stuff. Watching the council every Monday night took the desire out of us years ago.

I was talking to Jean Dickson coming back from Stevie Leacock's Award Announcement luncheon. We were on that very subject, "what is acceptable and what isn't in humorous books?" (You won't find Mordecai Richler's new book in the children' section of the library. His language is a little "salty.") I asked Jean if I could get away with using a bad word in one of my books. She said, "I don't know. What's the word?" I told her.

Have you ever tried to hitch-hike on Highway 400 at four o'clock in the afternoon?

I should have this problem.

Giving yourself a raise is a real tough call.
June 23, 1998

Last Monday Frank Mahovlich started his new job. He's now a senator. I'm not sure just what qualifications a person needs to take a seat in the Upper House, but I would think being able to skate real fast and knock somebody down would certainly be one of the main ones ... that, and being able to talk a lot. Frank said he was surprised because one chap droned on for forty-five minutes. He ought to watch Cable 10 on Monday night. A forty-five-minute speech at an Orillia Council meeting is considered an off-the-cuff remark.

But right off the bat poor Frank has to decide whether or not to give himself a raise. That's not fair. He's only been on the job a week and already they are trying to force him to take more money. I know the feeling because I used to work in personnel at Otaco. That was just before they closed it down and the property became a wildlife sanctuary. Every other day, I would get a call from the U.S. office and the president of the company would ask, "Do you want any more money today?" and I would have to call Eddie Beers, the union president. Eddie would say, "Of course not. Didn't I tell you yesterday that most of our folks are already making so much money that the Royal Bank wants to merge with us? By the way, how are you coming with our demands to go back to the sixty-hour week?"

But Frank will have to make the decision pretty soon. It must be nearly time for the Senate to take their summer recess. They can't leave it any longer, otherwise it could delay the next increase they have planned for the fall.

I have no idea what kind of money a senator makes. But I would think that they have to be in the same bracket as Conrad Black and columnists for the *Packet*. I don't know if a senator makes as much money as a member of Parliament, but I'm sure that they'd be close. I know Paul Deviller is doing all right. I saw him at the Leacock Dinner and he was wearing a suit.

Most people in Orillia don't understand how wage and salary programs work. At Otaco, we always based our salaries and hourly rates on the Dorr-Oliver-Long plant across the road. Whatever they made, we made half. If they got a holiday, we only had to work to noon. If they got a dental plan, we got a coupon for fifty cents off on a tube of Crest. (If you had no teeth, the company would exchange it for a complimentary nose-hair clipper.)

At Christmas time, we would all stand by the window watching the Long's people struggling home with their turkeys ... and not little twelve-pounders either. Sometimes it took three or four guys to lift one into the back of a truck.

One year all we got was a sparrow. But that worked to our advantage. The missus didn't have to slave over a hot oven all Christmas Day. She put it on an aluminum pie plate and stuck it in at 350 for fourteen minutes. The dressing was easy, she just ground up a soda biscuit, threw in a pinch of sage, and stuffed it up its bum.

I remember just before I got downsized (I was short enough as it was), we had a visit from the president. He gave us a stirring speech about what a bright future the Orillia operation had. I believe it was word for word from Neville Chamberlain's "Peace in our time" oration after he came home from Munich. That was the speech where he asked us to cut down on waste, like pencils, candles, and in particular, paper clips. The president had a thing about paper clips. I think he had the idea that we were smuggling them out and selling them to Francoz Metal next door. I miss him. I wonder what asylum he's in now.

Although I'm sure that the union didn't know it, but whatever new benefits they asked for, the folks on salary usually got them too. Tommy Scoular and I were on the company side. We would sit across the table hoping that they would hold out to the bitter end with some of their demands. The first time they let the dental plan drop from the table I almost cried. At our house, we only had one tooth amongst the four of us. If you wanted to use it you had to book it six weeks in advance. That's why there was only one person smiling in any of the family photos ... it was always the one who had the tooth.

But I'm glad that Chretien appointed Mahovlich to the Senate. That's what Canada needs, a hockey player running the country. At least when Frank does something stupid, we can blame it on his being hit on the head with a puck.

You'll never guess who I saw in the Mike's Milk Store.

Dealing with Elvis and Annis Stukas
July 21, 1998

Elvis is coming to town. I think this is a wonderful thing for Orillia and I'm so pleased that the organizers saw fit to honour a man who has been such an inspiration to the youth of our nation.

I saw him in person one time, I don't know if you knew that. Unfortunately I wasn't close enough to actually say hello or get his autograph or anything like that. I wouldn't have had the nerve anyway. I don't feel right asking a famous person to sign a program or invite him to drop around to the house to see our earwig collection. Some people can do that. They just march right up to an international star while he's eating dinner at French's Stand or having a beer at the First Hotel and talk to them just like they were normal people. Not that I haven't seen my share of celebrities, I just don't mention it. Some people have met hundreds of them. McGarvey has interviewed all kinds of world-famous people. He knows Clayt French personally and there were even rumours going around that he had once courted Jenny Lind, the Swedish Nightingale.

I'm not going to brag about the stars and starlets I've met, but I've been in the company of some pretty important people. Years ago, I was standing at a urinal in Maple Leaf Gardens and lo and behold, Annis Stukas, the general manager of the B.C. Lions, was right there beside me. I guess I should have asked him for his autograph but I was star-struck. Unfortunately in my excitement I turned to introduce myself and forgot what I was there for. I offered to rinse his pants out in the sink. While he was taking them off the cops came and took him away. That turned out to be a costly mistake for both of us. He spent the night in the Don Jail and I got fined two hundred bucks for operating a laundry without a licence. Apparently Annis was never seen in a public washroom again and whenever he goes to a football or hockey game he always has an empty milk bottle in his overcoat pocket. I never went back to the Gardens after that in case my name is on some list of troublemakers or something. You'd think that Annis would have been pleased that I recognized him, but he never even sent me a thank you note. On the other hand, what can you expect from some guy who's named after a secret body part?

I shook Mila Mulroney's hand once in the mall. That was long after the Maple Leaf Gardens thing and I had washed my hands and everything. I was impressed because she was good-looking and tall. Tall women have a strange effect on me. I'm not exactly what you would call a skyscraper myself and for some reason I always act like a jerk whenever some girl looks down at me. Of course I act like a jerk when I meet short women too, so maybe that's something I should be discussing with my therapist.

I was going to ask Mila for her autograph but when I reached inside my jacket pocket to get my pen, two big undercover Mounties grabbed me and tried to tie my neck into a reef knot. Brian rushed over to punch me out but when I offered to let him wear my Companion of Canada medal, he let me off with a warning. It was supposed to be forgotten, but I noticed that every time Doug and Linda Lewis had them over for dinner, my invitation gets lost in the mail.

Most folks I know act really goofy whenever a television star comes to town ... especially women. My wife walked right up to a big bruiser in a health food store in Midland and asked him if he was Tommy Hunter. He checked his wallet and sure enough he was. Then I felt obligated to talk to him about country music and I don't know anything about it at all. I asked him if Charlie Chamberlain was still running around with Marg Osborne and he just walked away shaking his head.

I'm certainly looking forward to seeing Elvis again. As a matter of fact, I'm going to try and arrange a private meeting with him. I have a few suggestions for his routine. I think after he does his quad he should do a backflip like Kurt Browning did in his TV special and then finish the whole thing off with a double klutz. It wouldn't hurt to change his music either. He should forget about all the classical stuff and skate to some more contemporary tunes, like Vaughn Monroe's "Racing with the Moon," Eartha Kitt's "C'est si bon," or even something by that guy from Graceland who's name escapes me for the moment.

The world is round? You've got to be kidding.

So you thought you knew history?
August 18, 1998

After too many hours in the hot sun last Canada Day, it struck me
that too few Canadians know the story of the discovery of North
America. (Except of course for the senior members of last year's
Council who were there to meet the boat.) On Canada Day, we
Canadians are a surprisingly patriotic lot. Although our patriotism
pales beside the Americans who worship their heroes with a zeal that
Canucks reserve only for their pets. Therefore it behooves me to tell
you how we were discovered and why our National Anthem should
be sung in Norwegian.

There have been many boring discussions as to just who were the
first people to set foot on our shores. I am not talking about the
aboriginals who were already here, having come across the Bering
Straits in hip-waders. Most historians agree that the first people to
arrive from Europe were the Vikings.

The Vikings were a peaceful group of Scandinavians, who rarely
left home except for their annual foray down the coast to rape and
pillage any hapless peasant who happened to be in their way.

Perhaps the most famous was the father and son team of Eric the
Red and his boy Leif the Lucky. Hollywood tells us that Leif looked
somewhat like Kirk Douglas with a glass eye, which makes you wonder
what Leif the Unlucky looked like.

In the summer of 1001 A.D., Leif set out in a dragon boat to catch
a show in the London Theatre District. (Dragon boats were so-named
because the figurehead on the bow resembled a dragon. It also
resembled Mrs. Leif, but you don't tell that to a guy with an axe.) Due
to a poor sense of direction and the fact that they were using a metal
compass and Bjarni, the coxswain, was wearing magnetized shorts,
they landed in Labrador. The liquor store being closed, they sailed
south to a land festooned with grapes and wild wheat. Historians are
uncertain exactly what this land was, but have narrowed it down to
either Nova Scotia (Vinland) or the farmer's field across the road from
the Bright's Winery bottling plant near St. Catherines.

There is almost no trace of the Viking civilization left in North
America, except for a football team in Minnesota and a few bottles of

Scandinavian vodka at the liquor store that can only be consumed while wearing a gas mask.

In May 1497, John Cabot, a Venetian sailor, (some say Genoan, but since he is dead, does it really matter?) set sail from Bristol with a crew of eighteen men and a cabin boy looking for China. They landed at Bonaventure, Newfoundland, which he believed to be the north-eastern extremities of Asia, or the south-western shore of Italy. (He wasn't great on geography.) He found no people, but did see snares set for game and notches on the trees, which indicated a primitive civilization ... or very tall beavers. Around the islands of St. Pierre and Miquelon, Cabot discovered the great fishing wealth of North America, a chain of Red Lobster franchises.

Back home, Cabot was royally received, honoured, and rewarded. He was given the title of Great Admiral, which Cabot thought was a television set.

In 1498, Cabot sailed again with two ships and three hundred men. Finding no trace of Chinese civilization, not even take-out, he loaded up with fish and furs and headed home.

The Bristol merchants were terribly disappointed and had him busted from Great Admiral to Poop Deck Superintendent.

Although his voyages never met the expectations of his backers, or his fronters either, they did establish England's claim to the north-eastern coast of North America and squid-jigging rights for years to come.

Sir Humphrey Gilbert, an English "sea dog" (so called because of his despicable practice of relieving himself on anyone with a peg leg) claimed Newfoundland in 1583. A settlement by Sir Walter Raleigh had failed previously when the Queen stepped on his cape which he had gallantly spread over a six-foot sinkhole, thinking it to be a mudpuddle.

Newfoundland remained a colony of England until 1949 when Joey Smallwood sold it to Canada for thirty-pieces of silver and a used Desoto.

There are very few native Newfoundlanders on the island today. Most have moved to Ontario where they are easily identified. They all wear yellow slickers, rubber boots and are the people who always show up at parties a half hour early.

Next week, the problems with Northwest Passage and why you should have a little check up every year.

Oh no, there's more of it.

A brief moment in time
August 25, 1998

The Northwest Passage was very important to England. Her efforts to find it resulted in a whole potful of explorers like Marty Frobisher, sailing around amongst the icebergs.

John Davis, who's great great nephew, Bill, would later screw up the Ontario Education System (Harris, Johnson, and Snobelin destroyed it), ventured north in 1586 to the strait that bears his name. In 1602, George Weymouth discovered another strait, but not being all that swift, forgot to name it. By the time he remembered, Henry Hudson had named it after himself.

I shouldn't suggest that Hudson was a bit of an egotist, but he did name a bay, a river, a car, a department store, a coat, and a blanket all after himself. They were finally forced to set him adrift in a rowboat to give someone else a chance.

Henry was an accomplished mariner. In the employ of the Dutch East India Company, he discovered and claimed the Hudson River in New York for Holland, as well as Manhattan Island. Later Peter Stuyvesant would buy Manhattan from the Indians for twenty-four bucks worth of costume jewellery ... about what you'd expect from a man who's idea of *haute couture* is a pair of wooden shoes and baggy pants.

The following year, Hudson, with a crew of twenty-three men sailed into Hudson's Bay and then on to James Bay (probably his middle name).

By this time, the bay was icing over and they were forced to winter on shore. Supplies were dangerously low and once the Kraft dinner was gone, the crew mutinied and set Hudson, his son, and eight of the heavier eaters adrift in a boat. Nothing was ever heard of their fate, although a Hudson's Beauty Salon was discovered in Orillia, Ontario, in the 1950s.

Not to be outdone, King Francis decided to send a French ship to horn in on the gold that Spain was yapping about. The Spaniards were much smarter than the rest of the Europeans: they went to Florida and stayed at the Fountainbleu. Frannie's expedition was under Jacques Cartier, a riverboat captain from St. Malo — which makes about as much sense as sending one of the Montgolfier brothers to pilot a moon rocket. By the time Jacques reached Newfoundland, there were so many ships sailing by St. John's they had to put up traffic lights. As he sailed through the Straits of Belle Isle, he was heard to remark that Labrador "must have been the land that God gave to Cain." Which is why France didn't try to scoop it until someone found iron up there.

He later sailed to Prince Edward Island, pausing just long enough to catch a matinee of "Anne of Green Gables," before heading up the coast of New Brunswick to waste a couple of hours at the Reversing Falls, the Magnetic Hill, and a few other tourist traps. Here they met a band of Indians who were glad to trade their furs for trinkets. The trinkets unfortunately fell apart on the way back to the Indian village, but the hair fell off the pelts once the wind blew on them. All in all, it was a pretty even deal all round.

On the banks of the Gaspé Peninsula, Cartier planted a cross, watered it, and claimed the land for France, naming the peninsula for the noise the king made when he got the tab.

In May 1535, Cartier took three ships up the Gulf of St. Lawrence, hoping to find a land that the natives spoke of as rich in gold and silver. Historians now believe it may have been the Windsor Casino.

Where the river narrows at what is now Quebec City, he found the Indian village of Stadacona, ruled by the great chief, Donacona, and his two daughters, North and South Tonawanda. After a sumptuous lunch of German shepherd and pemmican, they continued on until they came to Hochelaga (Montreal), an Iroquois village that was at war back then and still is.

The expedition was somewhat of a disappointment for Cartier and he packed up and sailed back to France. This time taking Donacona and four other Indians with him by trickery. The Indians thought they were going on a boat tour of the Thousand Islands.

Another expedition was not taken until 1541. This time to attempt a settlement. It failed. I would tell you about it but I'm getting as bored as you are.

In spite of his failure to settle, Cartier's achievements were of great importance to Canada. He discovered the major artery to the country, a river of such importance that they later named a fish market after it.

So where are we today? The Vikings are in Minnesota, the French and the English are still arguing over who owns what, and a route to China is no longer that important, since all the Chinese live in Vancouver.

Memory is the second thing to go.

Excuse me Tom, what was I saying?
October 6, 1998

As I approach my dotage (a state or period of senile decay marked by decline of mental poise and alertness — called also second childhood — Webster) it occurred to me that I am not quite as bright as I once was. Since I was never the sharpest knife in the drawer in the first place, you can imagine how disconcerting that must be. As I was saying only yesterday to my friends ... I seem to have forgotten their names at the moment, but I'm sure I will recognize them if I see them. As I was saying ... what was I saying? Oh well, it will come to me.

I've been noticing lately that I'm getting old. I've always had an excellent memory and at one time I could remember a person's name all afternoon and would only forget it when I had to introduce them to someone important. Once I was talking to a lady and the mayor came by. I said, "Ken, you know ... aah, I'm sorry, I've forgotten your name." She said, "Queen Elizabeth." I was so embarrassed. When I left, they were into the fisticuffs. Liz tried to sit in his chair.

This actually happened to me. I read an article on word association. After that, whenever I would meet a person I would try to think of some word that would remind me of his or her name. There was this guy I had known for years at St. Paul's and someone else I knew came up to us. I said "You know Dave Prophet." and Dave said "My name isn't Prophet, it's Deacon." Well didn't I feel like a stupid ass? I knew it was something religious. It turned out later that it didn't matter anyway. He thought I was Craig Sarjeant.

Why is it that our memory fails us whenever we need it, but all those little embarrassing things that happen to us come back on a regular basis? I already told you about wetting my pants in a boy scout parade, but something like that comes back all the time, like every twenty minutes.

Horrible things that happened years and years ago come back regularly to haunt us. Everybody else that was involved has long forgotten it but it's still there in our mind and pops up every time we meet the other person. For instance when I was 15 or 16, I was walking home from school and a neighbour pulled over up ahead of me. I thought he recognized me and I climbed into the back seat of his car. He was smooching his secretary. That was forty-five years ago and I know he still remembers it. Well, I guess it would be hard for him not to, I phone him two or three times a day, just to remind him.

But memory is a problem for us old guys and I think it has little to do with health or our I.Q. I believe that the reason we have so much trouble recalling names and other important things is because our heads are filled to the brim with useless junk. For instance, I can remember the Pythagorean Theorem: "The square of the length of the hypotenuse of a right-angled triangle equals the sum of the squares of the lengths of the other two sides." Now what possible good is that to me? Not only that, who cares? I've got too many other things to worry about. With Bill Clinton fooling around with Monica Lewinsky, I've got time to worry about some Greek playing with triangles 2,500 years ago? That theorem has been taking up space in my brain since 1952 and I haven't used it once. Not only that, what if it's wrong? Has anyone ever sat down and added them up?

All kinds of things I was taught in school turned out to be a mistake and my mind is cluttered with this stuff. My grade 5 teacher, Miss Holtzman, told me that Columbus discovered America in 1942 or 1492, I forget which. He didn't. (Once I asked her if I could go to the washroom and she said, "No. Stick it out until noon hour." And when I did I got the strap.) My mind is filled with all kinds of useless information, including that last gag.

I can recite Wordsworth's "Daffodils" and I don't even know what a daffodil looks like. I know they are yellow, but so are tulips. What if I'm wandering lonely as a cloud reciting "Daffodils" and I'm looking at some Dutchman's garden?

When Harris and Johnson get finished lousing up the school system, maybe they should appoint Snobelin or some other scholar to clean the junk out of the curriculum

Oh great! Here comes my neighbour and I can't remember who he is. Thank heavens his name on his shirt. I can almost make it out. It's T-o-m-m-y, that's it.

"Tommy, Tommy Hilfiger, come on in."

Just once more, Sophia, then I really must get some sleep.

That Jim Foster is just dreamy
August 4, 1998

Last Monday night I was in my favourite dream, the one where Sophia Loren and Jane Russell are fighting over me, when I was rudely awakened by my wife shouting out the window "Hey youse kids, don't go warpin' any more boulders at that there varmit." (My wife was raised in the hills of Coulson. I am trying to recreate the peculiar speech patterns of the hillbillies from that area.) Suddenly wide awake and wondering how I ended up in bed with Elly Mae Clampett, I asked the missus what in hell was going on.

Apparently some of the brighter kids in the neighbourhood were throwing stones at a skunk in the culvert across the road. Had it not been two o'clock in the morning, and had I not been wearing my bunny rabbit pyjamas with the feet in them, I would have gone outside and explained to the young chaps that people who hurl rocks at skunks are on the same intellectual level as a zookeeper who sticks his arm in a tiger's mouth to check for cavities.

Annoying a skunk is a lot like asking a politician to say a few words at a public gathering. You'll regret both long after they have gone.

The kids were polite enough and headed home to shave their heads or whatever it is that teenagers do these days.

Fortunately I am not considered a threat by the smelly little creatures. (I'm talking about the skunks now.) Either that, or they figure that I've become so roly poly over the years that they could out-run me. I realized this several years ago, when I was a handsome young bachelor. I had just walked out the door of my apartment building and one of the little darlings was six feet from the end of my nose. (I have no idea whether it was a little boy skunk or one of his sisters. It didn't seem particularly important at the time.) But he/she just turned and scurried away chuckling. I used to dress myself in those days ... enough said.

For some reason, the Orillia skunks seem to be bolder this year. I suspect that they have come to realize that any city whose citizenry worship a bunch of lunatics dressed in sequined Elvis pant suits must be on drugs and of little danger to anything but themselves. (Even the *Packet* last Monday was devoted to these relics of a lost civilization. Had the U.S. taken the opportunity to bomb Medicine Hat that weekend, the news would have been relegated to page 12, just after the comics and before the ads for the girls who will talk dirty to you until your credit card explodes.)

Just a few hours before the rock-throwing incident, I had been at the Leacock Home for the reading sessions. A skunk showed up to hear Dan Needles. Fortunately the girls at the door refused him admission because he was too cheap to buy a festival button. I didn't see him really, but like a weightlifter who has neglected to drop by the deodorant section of Shoppers, you know he's there. But just in case the skunk was malingering outside to get an autograph, I pushed Neil Ross, the guy who plays Leacock, out of the tent. The rest of us hid behind the tent flap and sniffed.

Dan Needles was superb, although his humour was overshadowed by McGarvey's remark that he remembered something that had happened forty years ago when he was 17. Based on Pete's twisted understanding of mathematics, I should be getting ready to start public school this September.

But I digress: Sunday night, Sharon and I were standing outside watching a handful of Elvis persons bail out over the Casino, (which sure beats lining up along Atherley Road for hours on end) when we realized that the neighbourhood skunk had also decided to catch the show. It's hard to keep your mind on the sky when you know that one of God's little creatures is lurking in the ditch waiting to tear your leg off. I don't know what skunks eat, but I would just as soon it not be me.

I am not afraid of wild animals exactly, but I'm not going to take any chances. Whenever I walk along the Lightfoot Trail, I always carry a big stick just in case a wolf or a puma is lurking in the underbrush ... or behind one of the piles of dog dirt that some of the local pet owners feel helps beautify the landscape.

My wife is afraid of snakes. They don't frighten me at all. Well, except last week when a black mamba slithered up our driveway. It was green and yellow and nearly a foot long. I wasn't scared really, but just in case, I stayed in the car until the paper girl came and chased it away.

Really Sophia, just once more. I have to get some sleep.

Another romance down the drain?
February 23, 1999

I'm going to have real trouble with this column. I have to keep it hidden from my wife. Normally I run my columns by Sharon to make sure that I haven't used a word in the wrong place, like typing "existentialism" when I mean "exoerythrocytic" — a mistake that some of the other columnists make all the time, I might add. Professional ethics won't allow me to mention their names; nor would I, Kate and Pete being friends of mine. What I might do is try to bribe the paper girl to somehow lose our *Packet* in the bushes, which could be a little difficult since we only have one bush and it's under a foot of snow.

I don't know how to tell you this but — I'm in love with Sophia Loren. I can't help it. People who are victims of unrequited love will understand. Sometimes a great love has no rhyme or reason. It's just there even though you know that nothing will ever come of it. (McGarvey had this thing about Marjorie Main and on their wedding night made Eileen wear a Ma Kettle mask.)

I tried to forget her (Sophia, not Ma Kettle) and had been doing so well, I rarely thought of her, except as I woke up in the morning, or when I was drifting off to sleep, maybe a dozen or so times during the day, but not often.

I certainly wasn't a wacko like that farmer from the west who pestered Anne Murray all the time. I never bothered Sophia at all. I didn't phone her or hang around outside her villa. Oh, I may have sent a few snapshots of me in my birthday suit to her, but certainly not enough to cause her any problems or have me hauled in for a psychiatric assessment.

Once I sent her a loaf of Italian bread as a love token, but unfortunately it went through the local post office during the noon hour and the only thing that made it to Rome was an empty bag and a few crumbs. I thought I had finally gotten over this obsession: I was down to two tranquilizers and a bottle of Chianti a day. Then I turned on the TV to watch the Memorial Service for Wiarton Willy on Groundhog Day and there she was on channel 9 autographing a cookbook. Instantly I was madly in love once again. I could hear violins playing "Volare" in the empty corridors of my mind (there are several). My heart was pounding. I broke out in a cold sweat. There was a hint of oregano in the air. It was too much: I lost all control, tore into the kitchen, and stuck my nose right into a pot of spaghetti sauce. I was young and in love once more — and my nose was burning.

If I had known she was coming to Toronto, I could have arranged to be there. The Sophia Loren Fan Club didn't notify me. Although I suppose that's understandable since one of my snapshots somehow ended up in the mailbox of the club president, Sister Mary Margaret.

It was already too late to drive to Toronto when I saw her on TV. By the time I got to the bookstore, she would be winging her way to Rome, Milan, Paris, or one of those other Italian cities. Yet I had to let her know that I still cared, so I faxed her another picture.

I'm sure that I loved her from the first time I saw her in a men's magazine back in the late 50's. She was wearing a harem girl suit and she was ever-so-handsome. I would rather not get into that right now. She wasn't wearing an undershirt and I haven't got time for a cold shower. But the movie *Houseboat* was my downfall. After I saw her all dressed for the big dance, I knew I would never be the same again. She was wearing a gold dress and she was ever-so-lovely.

As I recall, Soph (I always call her that when we're alone) was in love with Cary Grant at the time. She threw a shoe at him. Apparently that's a good sign in Italy. If a girl throws a boot at you, you've got it made in the shade. Why she would waste her time with a bozo like Grant when a handsome young stud like me was available I could never understand.

But who knows what goes through the mind of a woman? I was saying that very thing to Don Lander and Joe Francoz at the Leacock Home yesterday and telling them about sending her my snapshot, but apparently they didn't have time to talk. Joe suddenly remembered a pot of stew he left on the stove and Don had to make a call to Venezuela. Alas, I'll probably never meet her. It just isn't in the cards. And so Sophia and Jim will never be. There will be no books written about us. There will be no movies. Our names will never appear in the *National Enquirer* or any of the other quality magazines.

Another great romance has gone down the tubes, just like Romeo and Juliet, Bill and Monica, Pete and Ma Kettle.

Peter, you devil.

Hair today — lobster tomorrow!
November 24, 1998

A week ago, all Canada was agog when it was announced that Cynthia Dale and Peter Mansbridge got married. (Isn't that a wonderful word, "agog"? It conjures up all sorts of visions — none that we can discuss in a family paper.) It must be difficult for celebrities to try and keep their personal lives away from nosy reporters. I have the same problem keeping my private life away from the newshounds here at the *Packet*. In my case it isn't my celebrity status and fame that attracts them — although that is probably part of it — it's envy. I'm sure that Peter and Cynthia would have liked to have been able to invite all their relatives and friends to the little church in Malpeque, P.E.I., to witness their nuptials, but you know how it is. Some mouthy cousin would just happen to mention it to a friend and she would phone Mary down the street and Mary would casually tell the lady under the next drier, and before you know it, the media would get wind of it and invade the place.

The first thing you know there would be cameras and reporters all over the pews. Then Joe Clark would expect to say a few words and everybody would fall asleep and Petie and Cynthia would have to tiptoe out over snoring bodies to hobble off to their honeymoon suite.

To be honest, I'm worried about the longevity of their marriage. It is another fine example of a May-December wedding. Cynthia is a young chick of 38, but Peter is an ancient crock of some fifty summers and a hell of a lot more winters. Such an age gap can be fatal if they ever get around to romancing instead of studying lines and reading the news. I know I was certainly worried when Sharon and I got married. She is many many years younger than I am and the likelihood of serious medical consequences arising from such a relationship was worrying. Fortunately that's all that did arise and the team of heart specialists that went along with us weren't called into service.

In a way I admire Peter Mansbridge, this is his third marriage and it must have taken a great deal of courage to try again when he knew in his heart that he would probably blow another. Peter's second wife was Wendy Mesley, you know. I never did know what caused the break-up, but I expect it was because he's bald. I know that the lack of hair is supposed to be a sign of virility, but we all know that isn't true. It was just something the movie magazines spread around to make Yul Brynner feel better. I'm sure you remember that in *The Ten Commandments* it wasn't old skinhead that the girls chased after, it was Charlton Heston. Although now that I think about it, Yul did have some hair. He had one big ponytail that stuck out of the side of his head like a lamprey eel on a bowling ball. (The ancient Egyptians were not exactly world leaders in the hair design department. The modern teenager of today would fit in quite well in their society.)

Whether Peter's lack of hair was the major factor in their eventual divorce, I really can't say, but I know his refusal to wear a jet-black Elvis wig on their wedding night was certainly a problem for Wendy. Every time she phones me, she mentions it.

I'm sure that it's not easy being married to a tall, handsome public figure — ask my wife — but when both the wife and husband are famous and beautiful, it must be doubly difficult. Cynthia is no slouch in the looks department. To be honest, I have never seen her act in anything. I know I should be watching the Canadian TV shows that she's been in, but I'm not all that fond of the CBC's dramatic presentations. Everything seems to be shot in Toronto or the Maritimes. It's either cops and robbers up and down Yonge Street, or some little red-headed girl from the East Coast who is having an affair with a lobster.

I never thought of that — maybe Cynthia and Peter are not there for their honeymoon at all. They are there to do another TV pilot for the CBC, "Cynthia of Green Gables." This time a beautiful young lady lawyer falls in love with a handsome TV anchorman from Antigonish and they live happily ever after.

Then one morning she's out wading and sees this particularly handsome, virile young lobster ... and he's got hair.

What kind of lunatic would invent a child-proof lid?

Foster seeks remedy for kid-proof lids
December 8, 1998

The other morning I woke up at 4:30 with the eerie feeling that something was missing in my life. I lay there perplexed for a few minutes mentally sorting through my list of things I was supposed to have to fulfil my life until I realized what it was. It was air. My nose was clogged up again. Yes, it was time once again for my annual winter cold. I always get one just in time for Christmas. (With careful maintenance and with a bit of luck I can keep it going until early July when it will be time for my summer cold, which lasts much longer.)

But this year, I decided that I just didn't have time for it. So I hauled myself out of bed and went looking for the Sinutabs. Unfortunately, by the time I opened the box, sorted out the night-time capsules from the day-time ones, peeled off the sticky paper that was there, apparently for my protection, and jammed a knife through the shrink-wrap and my finger to pop out a pill, it was too late. I had already died.

Now I'm not trying to pick on the drug industry, but aren't we carrying this safety business too far? We have plastic wrap on the Scope bottles and some sort of squeeze-pull caps that I seem to get backwards. I push when I'm supposed to pull and when I squeeze it, the Scope squirts out the top and splashes on the floor that Sharon just finished waxing. I have to quickly wipe it up with a towel and hope it dries before she finds out. In the meantime, my morning breath is eating the paint off the bathroom wall.

We have child-proof caps on aspirin bottles. If I have a Force Nine headache, I don't have time to run up to my son's house to get the kids to open it for me — I'm in pain here. Why can't they just go back to the old twist-off cap that worked for fifty years? Of course, they used to have those little tins of twelve. I could never open them either without dumping a half dozen on the floor. I never knew what side to squeeze. The can said push thumb here. I defy anyone to be able to do that. I had to pry it open with a knife and I cut my finger again.

Who was the wiener who designed the caps on the windshield washer stuff? If you are some sort of genius and can figure out how to get the top off, which now has some sort of tricky lockie thing on the top of it, you are faced with a foil seal that you can only get through with an ice pick or a jack hammer.

On the other hand maybe it's not all these safety devices. Maybe it's me. I guess it's all part of my in-born inability to handle the simplest contraptions. I admit I'm a prize klutz. Nothing seems to work right for me. I have yet to master the seatbelt latch. Why is it that other humans can just pull the belt across and snap it together? With me it's a major project. To start with, I have never had a seatbelt that stays inside the car. Mine all hang out the door. I get in and reach for the damn thing and it won't budge. Then I realize that it won't budge because it isn't there. It's outside dragging in the slush somewhere. By that time, I've already started the car and there are bells ringing and all the lights on the dash are flashing to warn me that if I don't do up my belt the cops will get me. Once I open the door and get the belt back inside, the clip won't fit into the lockie thing and I start jamming at it. It finally snaps in there, but so does my finger and now it's bleeding. It was already bleeding from the damn Sinutab shrink-wrap and the aspirin can. Now I have to go back into the house and get a band-aid. But I don't know where Sharon keeps the band-aids. They're not in the medicine cabinet, that's filled with her hair stuff, gallons and gallons of it. She only has one head. Why does she need forty-seven different hair products? Another thing, why do women go to the hair dresser and then come home and wash their hair? Why do women hate their hair anyway? I like my hair. I even like Mike Duffy's hair and he doesn't have any. I'm off the subject again.

My column is ruined anyway, so while I'm crabbing, I might as well get one more thing off things off my chest. We rented a movie — *Good Will Hunting*. I liked it, but right at the beginning I thought the TV set had somehow clicked off "VCR." We were right in the middle of an Acura commercial that's been running for weeks about some girl hi-jacking this guy to drive her all over the city. It's bad enough that we have to watch the movie promos before we get into the main feature, now we have to sit through a car commercial. I thought one of the advantages of renting a movie was no commercials. Now I'm renting the damn things.

Thank you for your kind attention but I can't crab any more. I have to go. My nose is running.

I thought Orillia crooks were a little slow.

What kind of crooks are we producing?
September 3, 1997

When is this province going to stop worrying about teacher-student ratios and start spending a few bucks to educate the people who really need help ... the poor criminals? Last week, some guy in Barrie slipped out of his handcuffs and escaped from the police. Then in a move that will guarantee him a chapter of his own in *Great Jailbreaks of the Twentieth Century*, he ran home and hid in the freezer. Now I haven't had much experience running from the law, but I would think that running home is not the sharpest move an escapee can make. It took years for the marshals to find Butch Cassidy and the Sundance Kid. One good reason for their success was they hid in Bolivia. They didn't run home and climb in with the frozen hamburger. Of course, there were no freezers in the 1890s, but even if there were I'm sure that the Frigidaire wouldn't be high on their list of hiding places. Freezers would have brought a whole new meaning to the term "hardened criminal."

"We've found Jack the Ripper, Chief. Right now we've got him in the microwave. What do you think ... about five minutes on Jet Defrost?"

I believe that such a dumb move by a member of our modern criminal society is a direct result of the weakness of the Ontario Public School System. It's time that schools started to do a better job. A course on evading the police should be something that's taught to kids at an early age, say Grade 2 — 4 at the latest.

"Class. Today we are going to learn where to go when you are on the lam from the fuzz.

1) Don't run home.

2) Don't climb into anything that locks from the outside."

(This is not a problem in the Separate School System. Francis Smith, an ex-cop, is on the Board. Francis would never send a kid out into the world without a proper education.)

Now that Dave Johnson is whacking big chunks out of the education budget, it's going to get worse. I heard on the CBC, that in a national scholastic test, Ontario students finished halfway down the list in reading, near the bottom in the science category, and dead last in escaping from the fuzz. The kid they tested, put a paper bag over his head and just sat there.

On the other hand maybe there is some logic in hiding in your own home. Nobody would think to look there. They got the guy in Barrie of course, but Barrie is an exception. The citizens down there are not that far up the evolutionary scale. They simply wouldn't be able to think of any place else. My son Paul lives there. I fear for the kids. If they ever decide to take up bank robbery as a profession, the cops will just wait on the front lawn until they come home.

Another thing: it wouldn't be a bad idea to send the Barrie cops back to Police College for a refresher course in basic coppy tricks. 1) If the criminal is wearing a cape, a top hat, and says his name is Houdini, don't use the toy handcuffs.

I have been following a series on A&E about the rise and fall of the Mafia Dons who terrorized the United States in the late nineteenth and the twentieth centuries. Canada has no organized crime. We got around the problem by appointing our hoods to the Board of Directors of the major banks. They are still crooks, but now they're supposed to be good for the economy. The Mafia wouldn't have had enough nerve to even try some of the stuff these guys actually get away with. The annual meeting of a Canadian Big Bank is the only gathering in the country where everyone wears a mask. Bank executives understand the big scam. Although the Bell Canada employee who came up with the idea of charging fifty cents to redial a busy number made them look like amateurs.

The average citizen has always had a fascination for big time criminals, especially the ones who's middle name starts with "the" — Salvatore "The Weasel" Pepperoni, Al "The Used Car Salesman" Palladini, Jimmy "The Mentally Disturbed" Foster. This type of professional gangster is usually easy to recognize. He is the guy who can go on eating his chef's salad while the guy next to him is being made into a wind instrument.

I think the general public would let these hoodlums get away scot-free because secretly we envy people who ignore the law and get away with it. Thank heavens we still have sensible people like Jean Claude Van Darn, and Arnold Swartzen... Swartsank ... Swart ... (You know who I mean, the big guy who makes Dolly Parton look under-developed). If it wasn't for them, we would still be at the mercy of the Capones, the Lucianos, and ... what was the prime minister's name who gave us the GST?

Have you ever seen Anne of Green Gables naked?

Holy Moses, we've got icons
October 17, 1997

Thank heavens, last week the Canadian TV networks finally rolled out their long-awaited national rating system to classify our TV shows. Little icons will show up in the upper-left corner of your screen to tell your children whether or not they should let you watch the next program.

This is wonderful news. For far too long, kids have had to listen to "Oh dear" and "Abner, did you see that?" or "How come you never do that to me?". Now, just by reading these little symbols, your children can decide whether the next movie, or even the next cartoon, is suitable for adults or whether they should just give you a box of crayons and send you to your room.

I can't begin to count the number of times I had to ask my sons, Tim and Paul, "What did that mean?" until finally, completely exasperated, they turned off the set, or sent me to bed.

I'm sure that you've read all about the new rating system. There are six little icons that will flash at you for fifteen seconds at the start of every program. Which wasn't too well thought out since 92 percent of all TV viewers are in the john, or poking around the fridge during the first critical moments at the beginning of a program. This also explains why they spend the next hour trying to figure out who the guy is in the grey suit.

The system:

"C" means it's suitable for urchins from 0 – 18. Which I think makes a lot of sense. There are several programs that a week-old baby and a teen-aged boy with three rings in his tongue could share, at least on an intellectual basis. I believe that "America's Funniest Home Videos" would fit in there somewhere, although it will almost certainly guarantee that the baby will end up in the slow learners class until he or she is on the old-age pension.

"C8" is programming acceptable for eight-year-olds to watch on their own. There will be no nudity, profanity, or sexual content, which means that none of them will watch it.

"G" means general programming and will contain very little violence and must be sensitive to themes that will frighten little children. Now that is ridiculous. I need those little kids there to comfort me whenever I watch spooky stuff. It's reassuring to have their beaming faces looking over the back of the couch saying, "It's only a TV show, gramps. There's no such thing as a Mike Harris."

"PG" is for general audiences and is likely to contain mild profanity and words that are offensive to small children, like "nap time," "clean your room," and "quit playing in the toilet." It may also contain brief scenes of nudity. Some care should be taken before deciding whether to allow your kids to watch these little peep shows. A quick flash of Pamela Anderson will do no harm, but I'm sure that a split-second glimpse of Roseanne Barr in the buff would do irreparable damage to a small boy's psyche and he will immediately apply for early enrollment in a Tibetan monastery.

"14+" is for kids over 14. I find this fascinating. There could be scenes of intense violence, nudity, sexual content, and frequent profanity. Children shouldn't be watching this stuff on TV. That's what school playgrounds are there for. I don't want to watch that stuff with a fourteen-year-old. All I need is some kid covered in Clearasil explaining what is going on on my own TV set.

"18+" is for us grown-ups. It has lots of violence, graphic language, and explicit portrayals of nudity and/or sex. This symbol was obviously meant for anything on City-TV after eight o'clock. Moses Znaimer is all for culture on Canadian TV ... especially if there is barenaked women in it.

And that's it. As usual, they didn't go far enough. We need to add a few more icons if we are going to properly evaluate TV programming. I have a few.

"RS" - "RS" means anything that starts off with Robert Stack talking about an unsolved mystery. The biggest mystery is why he wasn't fired years ago. The only time Robert Stack was able to change either his expression or his voice was during a scene in the old Elliot Ness series when Al Capone set his pants on fire.

"GR" - "GR" means Geraldo Rivera alert. It was bad enough that he interviewed yo-yos every afternoon and evenings, but now he's on channel 50 late at night, crying as if he really is mourning the death of Princess Diana, rather than using the tragedy as just one more way to make a buck.

but...

"BS" - Ah yes, "BS", the Parliamentary Channels ... no more explanation is necessary.

And finally, the most important symbol of all.

"FT" - "Fashion TV," which means that all women and children should leave the room, and let us old geezers study the latest fashion trends in peace.

And just exactly what weed are you serving today?

A medley of vegetable phobias
June 16, 1998

Have you noticed that lately there is an alarming trend in our finer dining places to serve salads and vegetable dishes made from members of plant families that not long ago we ploughed under, dug out, burned down, or sprayed with toxic chemicals designed to defoliate a jungle? Now I'm not condemning the practice, I'm all for something new. I just hope that their chefs have had the good sense to read Bill Kellers' latest book, *Weeds, Seeds, and Other Ways to Wipe Out Civilization*. Far too often I have found myself staring at a clump of stringy vegetation on my plate and wondering whether I'm suppose to eat it or take it to the lab at the Guelph Agricultural College for identification.

Saturday, at the Stephen Leacock Award Presentation Dinner at Geneva Park, I found myself in the awkward situation of facing a dish containing a number of green things that I had never seen before. Now I was reasonably sure I was supposed to eat it. On the other hand, I didn't want to chow down on somebody's corsage and then find out that everyone in the room was snickering at me. (You've all had one of those embarrassing incidents, I'm sure, like the time you wandered out of a shower drying your hair and your wife was hosting a Tupperware party.)

I kept my eye on Morley Torgov up at the head table to see what he was going to do with it. Morley's from the big city and has culture ... not a good idea. I forgot he's also a lawyer and lawyers will eat and drink anything. Finally I tried just a little piece off the corner. It was wonderful. The menu said it was a salad of baby lettuces and a whole bunch of other stuff like kiwis, strawberries and mango. I thought a mango was a dance where you try to slither under a ski pole without throwing your back out.

There was also hearts of palm and lemon dill vinaigrette. I didn't know what they were either, but I ate 'em. I pretty well had to — the cook was peeking through the doorway with his fingers crossed. But the really frightening part of the dinner was the vegetables ... baby red jacketed potatoes (they were great, although I had trouble getting the little buttons undone) and (now this is scary) a seasonal medley of vegetables. I am always afraid of anything called a medley. You never know what they might stick in there. Most of the time we eat Canadian.

Our national cuisine is not too adventurous. An exotic dish in a Canadian restaurant is green and wax beans boiled for a half an hour in the same pot. The seasonal medley of vegetables had yellow stuff in it. At first I panicked and thought it might be slices of turnip. Turnip is awful stuff. (Show this column to your kids. Let them know that they are not alone.) I still don't know what the medley was, but I had to eat it. I had no choice. I was sitting beside Mary Town and while she was cutting my meat for me, she said, "Now eat up all your vegetables or there's no dessert." The yellow stuff was pretty good. But just in case, I sent a sample away to Guelph. Mordecai Richler couldn't make it. They said it was his kidneys, but you never know, he might have eaten a medley.

It was a wonderful evening filled with much humour and wine. In fact the more wine I had the funnier things seemed to get. Finally I found myself giggling away all by myself and Sandra Stanton, the Grand Poobah of the Leacock Associates, sent me home in a cab.

I don't know when the Canadian Restaurant Association decided that the traditional fare was too bland and started to import all these weird fruits and vegetables from the Caribbean. I suspect that in Jamaica or one of those other places, they don't eat any of that stuff. Whenever they hold a state banquet in the islands, the seasonal medley of vegetables is peas and carrots, which they have to import from Canada because all their fields are filled right to the fence posts with the yellow stuff they sell to Geneva Park.

But we are starting to try more and more of these exotic dishes at home. Sometime this summer we have to have some folks over for dinner. It's sort of a pay-back type of thing. We sponged off them all winter. Sharon has been poring through a whole stack of recipe books and sample menus to try and impress them.

We might take a chance on something really wild. It will still be the same old beans, but this time we are thinking about taking a chance and buying a can that has pork in it.

Have you taken a good look at the people that pass you on the street?

The whole thing is alien to me
January 6, 1998

The more I think about this alien thing, the more I'm starting to look at some of my friends. I used to think that they were a bubble off plumb, but now I'm wondering if they didn't come here from some far-off galaxy ... probably from some planet of lower intelligence.

I know the general opinion is that a race that could travel all the way to Earth would have to be super-intelligent, but you don't know my friends. I suspect they were on their way to a liquor store on Venus, got lost, and were too stupid to ask directions.

I was watching Midday on CBC one day and they were interviewing Bob Fournier. Bob is a scientist from the East Coast and knows everything. I bet he can even program his own VCR.

Bob says that most of the technology on "Star Trek" will be quite attainable in the future, with the exception of the transporter. The transporter is the machine that breaks you down into molecules and reassembles you somewhere else. Apparently it will be able to break you down, but it won't be able to reassemble you into quite the same shape. Which is too bad really. I thought it would be a wonderful thing to have if you ever got picked up in the R.I.D.E. program.

Wouldn't that be great? One moment you are looking down the barrel of Sgt. Gerry Sharpe's shootin' iron and the next, you have materialized in your own bed. Of course, if you really had been drinking, you might materialize inside the mattress.

Bob says that if there is even the slightest chance that there are other beings out there, there is virtually no possibility that they would ever look like us.

All the hillbillies that have been abducted seem to agree that your average run-of-the-mill alien is a kind of green color with big red eyes, sort of like your husband, ladies, the morning after the Super Bowl.

Myself, I'm inclined to think that they would look like a toaster oven with legs. However, I'm guessing.

What if they looked like one of those slot machines out at Rama and in the heat of the moment, you shoved a loonie in an alien's mouth and pulled the handiest lever. You might hit the jackpot or be up in front of Judge Montgomery on a sexual assault charge.

Another thing, if you have no idea what an alien looks like, how would you know if you met one? I was walking down the main street one day and I thought that a parking metre said hello to me. I realized later that it was Jay Cody, but it could have been an alien.

I was going to bring the subject up at Harvey's the other morning. There is a bunch of guys who meet there every day to solve all the world's problems. It's more of a braintrust than a coffee club. Unfortunately, there is only one brain between the whole works of us and Bill Price borrowed it and went to Florida.

It scares me though that the Americans are trying to contact these aliens by sending messages by radio waves. A few years ago they sent out a space capsule with a drawing of a man and a women without any clothes on. If they ever do come here, they'll be landing at the Four Seasons Nudist Camp looking for the president.

If we have no idea what these aliens look like, and have no idea if they are friendly or not, why would we be dumb enough to invite them?

Knowing the Canadian Immigration Policy, if they landed up here we'd put them in subsidized housing and hand them a welfare cheque. Except in B.C., where they would be shot down like dogs.

What if they got the American invitation and came looking for a party? Or worse, what if they tried to take over?

In Ontario, if one of them showed up wearing plus-fours and golf shoes, we'd make him premier .

That reminds me. I am not one to knock tradition, but that three-cornered hat that Big Al McLean wears in the Speaker's Chair looks exactly like the one Q wore when he kidnapped Picard off the Starship Enterprise.

I think I'd better get off this subject, here I am suggesting that Mike and Al are aliens. Imagine that. Although now that I think about it, a month or so ago, Big Al couldn't get the Opposition to sit down and quit making all that fuss about the Omnibus Bill. When I looked up, they were all gone. He could have used the transporter.

Some things should not be tampered with.

New discovery had Foster "whining"
October 27, 1998

I was stunned to read the other day that scientists have come up with
another bonehead discovery. This time researchers in Kansas City have
developed a supplement packed with artery-protecting nutrients that
may be just as effective as a couple of quarts of cabernet in preventing
heart disease. This tampering with the natural order of things has got to
stop. I don't mind them mixing up new additives to give you an extra
hundred miles on a gallon of gasoline, or a disposable foot that will
automatically jamb itself in a solicitor-general's mouth whenever he gets
on an airplane. And I was pleased that they discovered Viagra to give
seniors a bit more mileage, although I myself should be good for a good
twenty or thirty years. That was truly a wonderful invention. There is
nothing so heart-warming as watching the boys from the Golden K
"high-fiving" each other every Tuesday morning.

But I strongly resent medical busybodies finding another excuse
to keep me from protecting my pumper with a half-decent bottle of
red wine. Just when I had Sharon convinced that running a
pipeline from the Bright's Winery in St. Catherines to a tap in our
basement was a good investment, they come up with a pill to make
red wine obsolete.

I'm sure that most of my friends would have the tap installed in
their kitchen or beside the lazyboy chair in the living room, but not
me. I think a trip down the cellar stairs three or four times every hour
will be good for my waistline. (My friends, as you probably have
heard, have a bit of a problem handling alcoholic beverages. They are
the seedy-looking people you find lying in the snow of the front lawn
of the liquor store at twenty below zero, waiting for someone to open
the door.) Not all my friends have that problem, some of them make
their own. You will never see them in a liquor store. They are the
folks lying in front of the wine-making stores at twenty below zero.

I remember the morning I first discovered that sipping red wine
was an excellent way to protect my ticker from more damage, and also
the reason why most Frenchmen live to 120, which is a pretty scary
thought when you think of it. I read it on the Health page right here
in the *Packet*. I believe everything I read in the *Packet* — except

Reed's articles on the Orillia council meetings. I think Reed must be confusing the sessions with one of Abbott and Costello's old routines.

If I recall, the article on the health benefits of red wine was put out by a company that produced red wine, which I thought was a remarkable coincidence.

The big corporations are very good about doing things like that. They are quick to publicize any information that suggests that using their product is good for you. That's why the Lambourghini dealers, when they announced their latest model can hit two hundred miles an hour in second gear, were quick to send out a little flyer to tell you that they now have an optional ejection seat that will toss you fifty feet in the air just before your car hits that dump truck. Their next project is to come up with a set of gas-powered tweezers to pick the gravel out of your bum when you land on the side of the road.

But when I first read that wine was good for you, I set up an appointment with Doc McAllister to see if he could write me a prescription to pick up a gallon or two and stick Blue Cross for the tab. Doc McAllister is my Health Care Professional. That is a new term that the government is now using to get us used to the fact that after their penny-pinching drives all our skilled medical people into the States, we will be rhyming off our symptoms to some bozo whose entire medical knowledge will be the instructions on the side of an aspirin bottle.

Doc said, "Why are you so interested in red wine? You didn't, by any chance, read the article that said a glass of red wine could have beneficial effects for people like yourself whose heart is as reliable as a politician's promise?"

"Of course."

"Then I guess you didn't read the second part that said three or more a day could put you on the endangered species list, and you'll end up lying on the ground in front of the wine establishment of your choice."

I took that to mean he wasn't going to give me a prescription, so I left in a huff, which is similar to a Lambourghini but it will only go twenty miles an hour — assuming it has a pretty good tailwind.

Christmas comes but once a year — thank God.

Thumb screws and mortgages? Bah!
December 12, 1995

Usually I am filled with the Joy of Christmas. Sugarplums dance in my head. I see elves and fairies. (Come to think of it, I only see elves on the way home from an evening of plotting the defence of this great nation over a barrel of Double Diamond at the Legion. The fairies I see all the time.)

But this year I am filled with dread and foreboding. It started this morning at the hour six, when my beloved announced that the world would come to an end unless we installed a genuine, needle-dropping Christmas tree, instead of the hairy broomstick that lives in a box in our basement.

Having the courage of a lion, I immediately said, "Yes, my dove," and rushed down to the basement to stick pins in a doll of her that I had made for just this type of occasion.

If the Lord had been thinking, He never would have been born in December. Why should I, a devout soldier of the Church, have to go out in the dead of winter, up to my nether cheeks in snow and sleet, just to satisfy the insane cravings of my demented wife?

First I phoned my bank manager to see if I could arrange a sizable loan to cover the cost of such a purchase. Unfortunately I forgot it was still six in the morning and caught him in the arms of Morpheous. (That's his wife's name. I know it's a man's name but you ought to see his wife — shaves twice a day.) Not only did he deny me a Christmas tree mortgage, he also foreclosed on my Thanksgiving Day Turkey loan to boot.

So I was forced to dig into my retirement investment portfolio: a cellar full of empty beer bottles. (I had planned on cornering the market and selling them back to Labatt's at fifty cents a crack.)

By the way, serious investors these days have "investment portfolios." My portfolio consists of thirty bucks squirreled away in an old sock.

I realize that this is no time to try and revamp the schools' mathematical curriculum, but shouldn't there be some sort of course available for a chap to at least be able to hazard a guess as to what height tree he should buy? Trees come in only two sizes: "Too short" and "Where's the damn saw ?"

I decided that I needed a tree exactly my height, (5'6" or 6'5", I can never remember which) if it was going to fit into our wrecked room. Unfortunately all the trees I saw were lying down, so I had to stretch out in the slush until I found one my length. Fortunately I was able to find one after only three hours, thirty lie-downs, and a near fatal incident when my parka hood filled with water.

I was supposed to buy a Scotch Pine. Since I don't know a Scotch Pine from a Manitoba Maple, I just picked one that looked like Bonnie Prince Charlie — only green.

When I got home, fifteen bucks poorer and with more needle marks than a Detroit junkie, I realized that only half of Charlie's needles were still on the tree, the rest were sticking out of my spare tire. By the time I got it downstairs into the wrecked room, there was only one needle hanging precariously from one of the lower branches. The other twelve million were up in my living room watching Oprah.

In trying to insert the tree into the child-proof tree holder, I broke off the only branch with a needle, so I had to Scotch tape it back on the tree. It looks quite nice really. A little scrawny, but nice.

It is a little scary, though, to realize that there are more Conservatives in the House of Commons than there are needles on my Christmas tree.

Incidentally, why can't a society that can put a man on the moon and caramel into a chocolate bar without leaving welding marks come up with a tree holder that works?

We've got one of the old ones with the thumb screws. I'd like to use the thumb screws on the guy who built it. By the time I got it up, the room was covered in sawdust and my tree still looked like the Leaning Tower of Pisa after a wine-tasting party.

I'm always a little dismayed when Sharon asks me to help out around Christmas. I'm not really a Christmassy kind of guy. I'm the only one I know who liked Scrooge before he saw the ghosts, and when he went nuts on Christmas morning and gave away all his money I cried.

I felt the same way when I found out that Madonna wasn't a virgin.

Now there's an interesting thought. I read a couple of years ago that Madonna spends a hundred grand a year on underwear. I wonder if she would forego a couple of sets of drawers in '96 and buy me a half-decent artificial Christmas tree.

Charlie Dickens was wrong.

Alive and well and living in Orillia
December 19, 1995

Let's just clear up some misinformation here. Most people are under the impression that Charlie Dickens' tale A *Christmas Carol* was set in London, England.

Not true. It may come as a bit of a surprise, but Ebenezer Scrooge was a partner in the firm of Scrooge and Marley, Chartered Accountants, on Mississaga Street, here in Orillia. Well think about that. Outside of Sodom and Gomorrah, where else could you find a butcher shop open on Christmas morning?

Can you imagine if that happened today? I mean that whole *Christmas Carol* bit ... some little kid running by Scrooge's window, and old Ebie hanging out the window hollering, "Hey you. Yes you boy. What day is it ?"

Nobody can accuse old Scrooge of being too bright. It's Christmas morning ... Cratchit and those other weasels at the office, all O.P.S.E.U., for heaven's sake. Old Ebby just paid them time and a half for Christmas Eve, double time for Christmas, time and a half for Boxing Day. a floater for Monday. They're supposed to work Thursday and Friday, but Cratchit has to take Tiny Tim to the orthodontist on Thursday. Friday is old lady Cratchit's birthday. So he might as well give Bobby the day off 'cause the old dolly will be phoning every half hour saying "When are you coming home?" What does Scrooge care what day it is? It's a hell of a day no matter what day it is.

Oh she was a winner, old Mrs. Cratchit ... a quart of gin a day, and that Martha, the oldest daughter ... slept in more beds than George Washington. The original good time that was had by all, that one.

Where was I? Oh yeah, Scrooge hollers out, "Hey you, yes you boy. What day is it?"

Today the kid would shout back, "What day do you think it is grandpa? Where have you been, smoking grass? Get away from me ... you on drugs or something?"

Of course the papers would get a hold of it and CKVR would run it on the Very Raptured news.

Police were called today to investigate the attempted abduction of young Leroy Fezziwig by local businessman Ebenezer Scrooge of the firm of Scrooge and Marley. Scrooge, according to an eyewitness, was seen hanging out his window wearing nothing but a nightcap and what appeared to be some sort of dress. Young Fezziwig, obviously upset by the incident, said the old guy tried to give him a loonie to come around the corner and see what he had hanging in his window.

Priscilla Pumphandle, President of "Mothers Against Old Geezers in Nightshirts," said today, "We'll show him what's hanging around the corner. It will be him the old pervert."

Meanwhile local police have been swamped with calls from residents demanding protection from this sex maniac who has been prowling the streets for years.

"I seed the old goat a-spying at me through my bathroom window." said ninety-four-year-old Maggie Muggeridge, "I could see the lust in his eyes."

The prime minister, Jean Chretien, announced this afternoon that he will call Parliament back from their annual six month winter vacation to reinstate the death penalty.

From Paris, the prissy little guy with the ponytail and the fan has announced that a whole new line of nightwear called "Ebenezer's Body Squeezers" will be in the stores by Monday morning.

In the meantime, Scrooge remains locked in the beer fridge at the Legion awaiting psychiatric evaluation.

Some day I'd like to write an update on old Scrooge, because he didn't come out of it all that badly. Granted Belle, the honey he used to run around with, dumped him. Something about wearing her underwear. But let's look at him now. He's got all kinds of money — 150 years old and on an indexed pension since he was 65. A good job at Canadian Tire, a chalet up by Collingwood, hot and cold running maids. A great catch for some widow. She wouldn't have to cook. Old Ebby ate gruel all his life. He'd think a TV dinner was French cuisine. And besides, what woman wouldn't go rangy over a guy in a see-through nightshirt?

The only drawback I can see — he's up half the night running around with a bunch of ghouls and spending a one hundred bucks a week on Geritol and vitamin E.

More bad news for the T.S.E.

S. Claus Corp takes over EasterBunCo
December 15, 1996

The financial world was shocked today by the announcement of yet another corporate takeover. This time the giant S. Claus Corp has purchased controlling interest in philanthropic rival, EasterBunCo.

In a press release, president and CEO of Claus Corp, Christopher Kringle, revealed that talks have been going on secretly for some weeks and a final deal was hammered out late last evening at the warren of E. Bunny. Bunny, apparently recuperating from a number of hammer blows, was unavailable for comment. His hearing also seems to have been affected. Surgeons at T.G.H. say that his ears appear to be 6" to 8" longer, as if someone had been pulling on them. In a typed and unsigned statement, Bunny said he has been considering retirement for some time and plans on spending the next few days in a pot of boiling water, along with some carrots, peas, and parsley to look at his options.

According to Kringle, Claus Corp plans no major restructuring of their latest acquisition, EasterBunCo. However, a joint statement by Tinker Bell — president of the International Union of Elves, Gnomes, Fairies, and Sprites — and Thumper Hare — Chief Steward of the Pookas, Bunnies, and Cottontail Employees Association — suggests that hundreds, if not thousands of their members could be thrown out of work. Said Thumper, "The egg-decorating division of EasterBunCo is on notice of lay-off, and Colonel Sanders has been seen sniffing around the laying-hens complex." Bell is even more concerned, saying that his membership has already been decimated by Claus Corp's recent decision to buy off-shore from Asian toy manufacturers and by the subsequent down-sizing of the North Pole plant. "Last year alone we lost 4,200 elves in the hobby-horse and pull-toy division. Since the plant is located at the North Pole and does not appear to be part of Canada, or for that matter, anywhere, it is not covered under the Ontario or Federal Labour Relations Acts. Claus laid off our members without proper notice and with no regard to the seniority provisions of the contract. Some workers have been with the firm since the early 1700s and were simply turfed out in the snow. To add insult to injury, in his latest address to our membership, he told us where we could stick our collective agreement."

If the reader will remember, the Claus Corporation has been under investigation for some time by the T.S.E. after last year's ruthless takeover of Tooth Fairy Inc. It was later disclosed by the R.C.M.P that evidence suggests that Kringle may be in cahoots with both the Ontario Dental Association and the Canadian Denturist Association in a dastardly plot. They plan to buy all the little children's teeth for a quarter, make them into a full set of dentures, and peddle them to seniors at 2500 bucks a crack. The investigation continues.

The public has been concerned for some time about Claus Corp. Although most appreciative of the gifts, citizens questioned why a major corporation would give away countless thousands of toys and fondue pots each year for no apparent reason. There was also some concern as to where the money was coming from to fund such an enormous project. Later it was discovered that shortly after a home had been visited by this self-proclaimed jolly old elf, the family reported the theft of silverware, VCRs, CD players, and unopened beer and liquor.

The Ontario S.P.C.A. are also looking in to a number of complaints of alleged mistreatment of eight tiny reindeer. According to witnesses, the animals have been seen on numerous occasions hauling some big fat guy across the sky in a sleigh. From the descriptions, the driver appears to be either Kringle in a fur suit, or Roseanne Barr in a red slip.

It has also been suggested that Claus may be using some sort of controlled substance in his pipe. According the Narcotics Control people, anyone who flies through the air with no coat and his nose three feet from the exhaust pipe of a reindeer is obviously smoking something.

So far, Paul Martin, the federal finance minister, has not commented on whether the government will approve this latest buy-out. According to Reform leader Preston Manning, we are not likely to hear much until Martin sees how he makes out Christmas morning.

In the meantime, citizens are asked to keep an eye open for any strange sleighs in their neighbourhood and to make sure the missus keeps her nightie buttoned right up to the top.

Another year of botched Christmas gifts.

I hate to complain, Santa, but ...
December 2, 1998

Dear Santa,

I'm putting this year's letter in the *Packet*, just in case Mr. Gardiner our mailperson, is still on strike and parading up and down in front of the post office, and my list is being held as a hostage.

(Richard Needham said, "The ghastly thing about postal strikes is that after they are over, the service returns to normal." That has nothing to do with Christmas: I threw that in for nothing.)

I don't know what happened last year, but either you can't read or you need new glasses. I know you don't have time to read every little boy and girl's letter and sometimes your elves have to help. If possible this year, please direct mine to some fairy who can read English. I distinctly remember writing that I badly needed a pair of cords. Cords are pants, Santa. What I'm going to do with two piles of firewood I have no idea. We haven't even got a fireplace. I could carry it over to my son's house, he's got one. But last year he asked you for a new chair and it got stuck in the chimney. Don't you measure those things before you ram them down somebody's smokestack? We had to pull down the whole chimney. It was a hell of a mess. By the way, you'd better count your reindeer. I don't know if that's what was in there, but it had antlers and a red nose.

I hate to complain, but do you know where I can get rid of thirty pairs of socks? I know for sure I asked you for a new wok. My wife went at our old one with an ice pick, and now it won't even hold water let alone stir fry. As for the socks, I can't even give them away. They look like they might be size eighteen, and bright orange. They may be all the rage at the North Pole, but nobody will wear them here in Orillia, and Orillians think a tie with a fish on it is *haute Couture*.

This may sound picky, but last year I left you a beer along with my list of last minute items in case you had some stuff left over. I thought a beer would have been a reasonable gift in exchange for a new VCR or something, but apparently you felt it necessary to lift the better part of a case of twenty-four ... and the bottle of Johnnie Walker that I was saving in case Chretien and Deviller showed up on Christmas morning. There were also a few cookies on a plate that we thought might tide you over until you got back to the Pole. I don't know why you felt entitled to scoff the leg off our pre-cooked turkey. And that cup of brandy in the fridge was for the plum pudding. I hope you enjoyed it because we had to eat the stuff cold sober.

I don't know who does the housework at your house, Claus, but I'd appreciate it if you would take off your big boots before you march across our rug. My wife was furious. We had company coming and you left big clumps of mud and shingles all over the carpet. She tried to clean them up with one of those spray cleaners, but that didn't work. When our company came, it looked like the Russian army had held manoeuvres on our living room floor and the house smelled like Lysol. We tried to drown the smell with a scented candle, but it was worse than the Lysol and we had to eat dinner with the doors open.

It's customary, Nick, to place the gifts under the tree, not fire them all over the living room hoping the odd one will land in the general vicinity. The chainsaw landed on the cat. (Incidently, I asked for a gold chain like the swingers wear in exotic places like Udney and Sebright.) Now even Christmas music on the radio sends her cowering under the bed, and our vet bills are staggering.

Here's my list and for heaven's sake, get it right this time. Jobs are scarce: you don't want to be out looking for work this time next year.

I still need a pair of cords, but they seem to have changed the sizes again. I usually wear pants with a thirty-inch waist, but this time make them forty-eight inches and I'll tie the tops together with that old rope you gave me last year. (Yes I asked for rope, but I wanted the kind with a bar of soap hanging on the end of it.)

I need some underwear. The stuff you left last year didn't stand up: the lace fell off the legs and there was no fly in them. I know Maude Arnems had a sale last November, but use some common sense, man.

That's all I'm going to ask for for myself. I wonder though if you could do me a favour. My uncle Alan cut some of his toes off in a lawnmower fight a few years ago. A month ago I read that Mike Harris has six toes on one foot. Would it be possible for you to sneak into his bedroom, lop one off, and stick it on my uncle? Don't feel bad about hurting Mike. He wouldn't think twice about doing it to you. My uncle will sure be happy Christmas morning when he puts his socks on ... especially the orange pair I'm sending him.

Little Jimmy Foster

Never go into the basement without a map.

One woman's junk is another man's ...
January 7, 1997

Women, although they are quite lovely and occasionally show signs of a primitive intelligence, have almost no comprehension of the basic laws of the universe. For example, my wife does not understand Archimedes Fourth Law of Space, which says "A basement can hold only a basement's worth of clutter." I believe Archie discovered this law while in the bathtub with Euclid.

I noticed this on New Year's Day, while I was taking down the Christmas tree. Well I didn't physically take down the tree per se — whatever that means. Apparently, my idea of shoving the tree, decorations and all, into a box and throwing it down the basement stairs was not considered practical. Besides I'm not allowed to touch the fragile stuff. My sole contribution to the Christmas tree project was to lie on the couch and bemoan the fact that I spent New Year's Eve nursing a couple of beers and never even caught a glimpse of a cop on the way home. As a matter of fact, I haven't seen one for two years and have started to suspect that this whole R.I.D.E. program thing exists only in the mind of some yokel from Arkansas who gets picked up by aliens every Tuesday.

I digress. Apparently it is against the law to throw out boxes. I never knew that. I thought that once the boxes were empty, you simply threw them in a garbage bag and the city made something useful out of them.

But my wife says we have to save them just in case we run across a Christmas gift next year that will fit into one of these boxes. The fact that the gifts come in boxes in the first place seems to have escaped her. While trying to find a hole to put this year's boxes in, I had to remove last year's boxes to make room for the current models, which I can't throw out because you can never have enough boxes.

Our basement is full of her useless junk. We have Christmas decorations down there that were old when the three wise men were hitchhiking to Bethlehem.

I cleaned off half the shelves and piled all the stuff on top of the freezer. Some of the stuff has to stay there because it is mine. I brought it with me when we got married. I don't dare throw it out because I'm still on probation. Besides, it's all valuable. A lot of my dishes are made out of a substance called Melmac which was considered crystal back in the Fifties.

There is a set of beer mugs made out of old beer bottles that my father gave me. Apparently they give you the illusion that you are drinking beer out of a bottle. The logic escapes me. I forget who made them, but I doubt that his name ever comes up whenever fine art is being discussed.

There is a cast-iron frying pan down there. At least I think it's cast iron, there's a substance stuck all over it. I think it may be an omelette that was slightly overdone, but I'm not sure because I let it soak a few days and it rusted. I can't throw it out because somebody told me that you can't beat a cast-iron frying pan.

There's a whole bunch of refrigerator drawers. I don't know where they came from. They don't seem to fit the fridge that's down there. Besides it has it's own drawers — although they aren't in the fridge because I took them out one day to have the mould examined at the Science Centre, and I couldn't get them back in.

I've got all kinds of empty jars that someone asked me to save for them, but I think they died or moved away. I have to keep them because someday I might do some pickling. I think I saw some old cucumbers in a box. Either that or it's more decorations.

I've got two dish draining racks that will be valuable some day. An old girlfriend told me that at her house she washed and God dried. I tell that to Sharon every week or so, but I think the humour is wearing thin.

There's an exercise bike that I haven't got around to using yet because the seat hurts my bum. If I can find a new seat, I'll probably ride miles. There's some barbells lying on the floor but I can't lift them. If I ever get in shape I'll use them, but right now I just roll them around the floor with my foot. My feet are now very muscular, but I'm afraid the rest of me has gone to seed.

There's two old lamps that I must have got at a garage sale. I'd throw them out but they weigh more that the damn barbells and I can't get them up the stairs.

I've got a suitcase full of heads, not real ones but some ceramic ones that were very big in the Sixties. I planned on selling them to a collector for a grand each, but I saw them in the Sears catalogue for $19.95.

I've got a whole bunch more stuff down there, but I can't take the time to tell you about it. I have to make supper and I can't get into the freezer. All my wife's useless junk is piled on it.

Thank heavens I'm an Elizabethan scholar.

Rushing to Shakespeare's defence
November 17, 1998

The other day, I came across an interesting bit of information about William Shakespeare. Apparently Bill was considered a hack writer by the literary giants of his day. Well all except for his friend, Ben Jonson, who was a bit of a hack himself. (His great grandson, Dave, went into politics and overnight learned all there is to know about education.)

I know just how Bill must have felt to be criticized by his peers. Several years ago when Brownie, Jim Lewis, and myself were just starting to scribble a few lines for *Oh Really Orillia*, some of the better known playwrights of the modern theatre, Neil Simon, Bernie Slade, and Woody Allen, were somewhat critical of our early efforts. It probably wasn't until our second or third year that we were finally considered on a par with the big three and it was close to the fifth or sixth year of our show before we surpassed them in quality, originality, and just sheer brilliance.

Shakespeare must have been devastated by their snobbery. But like all good writers he persevered and eventually wrote several plays that were fairly well accepted, although none ever received the critical acclaim of Brownie's "Man Smoking a Cigar" sketch in the '98 *Oh Really Orillia* show.

If I have any criticism of Bill's work, it's simply that he would have done so much better if he had written his plays in English, and maybe a yard or two shorter. When I went to high school, we had to study at least one of his works every year — not because they were all that exceptional, but because he had been dead over fifty years and the school board could use as much of his stuff as they wanted and not pay a dime in royalties.

In the 1950s, no normal teenager was capable of understanding a word of Will's plays without the guidance of a team of English Lit specialists who had dedicated their lives to trying to pound the love of great literature into us. Since there are only a few dozen of us scholars from that era who are still mentally alert and actually understand words like "forsooth" and "gazooks," I have taken the time to translate some lines from a number of his plays into everyday language.

Love's Labour's Lost, **The naked truth of it is, I have no shirt.** - (translation) If you don't have a blouse, lady, move to Ontario. You can go topless there.

Romeo and Juliet, **O Romeo, Romeo! wherefore art thou Romeo?** - Juliet is saying to her girlfriend, Bessie, "Have you seen that jerk, Romeo? I just got a call from old Doc Smithers. The rabbit died."

Henry IV, **Is it not strange that desire should so many years outlive performance?** - (translation) Did you hear Trudeau is going out with some girl in Grade 12?

Much Ado About Nothing, **Done to death by slanderous tongues** - (translation) Did you happen to catch Bill Clinton before the Grand Jury?

Julius Caesar, **This was the most unkindest cut of all.** - (translation) It's bad enough you cut it off, Mrs. Bobbitt, but did you have to throw it out the window?

Hamlet, **Something is rotten in the State of Denmark.** - (translation) All right, which one of you bozos left the Danish Bleu cheese in the hot sun?

Again from *Hamlet,* **This is the very ecstasy of love.** - (translation) No, Fred, the earth didn't move. The bed collapsed. You weigh nearly three hundred pounds.

King Lear, **Through tattered clothes small vices do appear.** - (translation) I hate to tell you this, your majesty, but the bum is out of your polo pants.

King Lear, **When shall we three meet again, in thunder, lightning, or in rain?** - (translation) Hey Kenny, when's the next meeting of the E.D.C.?

Macbeth, **Out, damned spot! Out I say!** - (translation) Oops, sorry Monica.

The Tempest, **Knowing I loved my books, he furnished me, from mine own library with volumes that I prize above my dukedom.** - That was Pete McGarvey saying to Eileen, "I don't suppose Foster brought back those *National Lampoon's* he borrowed two years ago?"

And finally, from *Much Ado About Nothing,* **Bait the hook well: this fish will bite.** - (translation) "Better run off a few more TV ads about our health and education programs, Mike. We've got an election coming up in the spring."

The Merchant of Queen's Park lives
March 2, 1999

Last year, the world was overjoyed by the confirmation of yet another Shakespearean play, Edward III. (There is still some controversy as to whether it's Ed the third, or Ed the one hundred and eleventh. When they figure it out I'll let you know.)

I remember so many happy hours when we were lads, searching through *Macbeth* or *King Lear* for the dirty parts. We were a disgusting bunch of bozos when I think about it. Yet in spite of us, Bill's works live on and will be here long after the scribblings of today's playwrights are so much landfill. Rather than let his writing style be lost in antiquity, it behooves me to emulate his phrasing. Or to put it another way — cash in on a sure thing.

The Merchant of Queen's Park

Enter Harrissio, Prince of North Bay, Davidio, Thane of Johnson, and Elizabeth, Duchess of Witmer.

HARRISSIO

Forsooth, I know not why I am so sad. It wearies me; you say it wearies you.

DAVIDIO

Odds bodkins, thou speakest in riddles. Why for art thou filled with despair? Ain't, I mean, aren't thee Premier of all the serfs from the edgemost lands of the French persons to the great plains where the gentle folk of the cowboy hats and funny boots think thee a buffoon? What more can a man whose only skill is thrashing his way fromst out a sand trap without doing harm to his kinfolk, hope to accomplish?

HARRISSIO

Thou dost speak truth, cousin, yet e'en so, I am filled with discomfort. My people dost not love me as once they didst. What say you, my pretty?

ELIZABETH

Fear not, my liege, I warrant that many of thy brethren still worship thee. Although I canst think of none offhand. Perhaps thou shouldst wander amongst thy people in disguise and hearest what they dost say of thy governing. Methinks thou will be surprised by their love.

DAVIDIO

Well spoken, sweetcheeks. Let us then don beggars' rags and tarry in the marketplace to hear the comforting words of thy subjects.

HARRISSIO

'Tis a plan. Then shall we meet on the morrow at sunup or 10:30, whichever comest first. Till the morrow then. *Exeunt.*

The morrow, quite early, about 11:30

HARRISSIO

We thankest thee, good Palladinio, for the use of thy limo. Forgetteth not to putteth in a chit.

Palladinio exeunts.

Gazooks, this is a seedy place. The hovels are overgrown with vines and all manner of strange vegetation. Wherefore art we?

ELIZABETH

The peasants call it, Forest Hill, m'lord. Tis home for the working class, Bank Presidents, University Deans, Dicky Dee salesmen, and scoundrels of that ilk. How now lads, what think thee of mine disguise?

DAVIDIO

Most clever, fair Elizabeth. Thy robe, tis mink? And thy garment, Ralph Lauren? Beshrew me, but thou hast a great bod.

ELIZABETH

Though art a saucy knave, Davidio. I lovest the way thou combest thy hair to cover thy bald pate. But verily, thee are right about mine raiment, I didst drag these rags from a dumpster at the Bridal Path Sally Ann. What ho, Harrissio? Thy breeks would tempt the very moon to hide its silvern head in shame. It is rare one sees such a devilishly clever pattern anywhere but on the blanket of a farmer's steed. Where didst thou get such a cloth?

HARRISSIO

I'faith, 'twas not from a nag's coverlet, lovely Lizbit, 'Tis a snippet from the red tartan jacket that Big Al McLean wears around the house to celebrate his heritage. But marry, shall we not approach yon bumpkin and ask him dost he love us? Tarry, good fellow, thou seemst a likely lad. What is thy name and how dost thou earn thy keep?

BUMPKIN

Nice pants! Forsooth, I am Conrad, of Black, and dost have mine own paper route. Who is yon oaf with his hair combed from back unto the front?

HARRISSIO

[covering his face with his ermine beggar's robe] Tell me, merchant, how say you to the workings of thy elected servants at Queens Park?

BUMPKIN

Good nose, I mean, good sir, I lovest them like my very own. *Exeunts in a black Ferrari.*

HARRISSIO

Ah, fair Elizabeth, we are yet loved by the common folk. Shall we then play nine holes before we close another hospital? And thee, Davidio, canst spare an hour from thy labours?

DAVIDIO

Alas, nay. I'm off to Queen's Park to choose a uniform for the ragamuffins in the school system. How say you to McLean tartan jackets, brown woollen plus-fours and a pinwheel hat?

HARRISSIO

Done. What say you, sweet Liz?

ELIZABETH

I say, all's well, that end's well.